When Adolf Hitler unleashed his Blitzkrieg on Western Europe, the Luftwaffe's famous dive-bombers were in the vanguard. The panzer armies received well-coordinated aerial close-support when they needed it and Germany's bombers relentlessly pounded the stunned Allies.

Following the capitulation of France and the fall of Belgium, Luxembourg and Holland, Britain stood alone yet continued to received the merciless attentions of the Luftwaffe's bomber fleet. From the end of the Battle of Britain in September 1940 to shortly before the invasion of the Soviet Union the following year, a huge strategic bombing offensive was mounted against Britain.

Wave upon wave of aircraft emblazoned with the Nazi swastika indiscriminately bombed civilian targets – devastating large areas of London, Belfast, Birmingham, Bristol, Cardiff, Coventry, Glasgow, Hull, Manchester, Liverpool, Plymouth, Portsmouth, Sheffield, Southampton and Swansea. More than 40,000 civilians were killed and more than one million homes in London alone were damaged or destroyed.

Yet the Germans never quite had the bomber force they had planned for – with projects such as Bomber B stillborn on the drawing board and the high-tech He 177 proving just as dangerous to its crews as it was to the Allies. The mighty weapon that had proved so appallingly effective during the Blitz began to suffer heavy losses against advanced Allied fighters and what remained was largely bled away during intensive operations on the Eastern Front, where it was often forced to fight at extremely low level in order to support Germany's beleaguered armies.

As the Luftwaffe's bomber units fought on with hasty upgrades and modifications of outdated machines, there was some faint ho bombers might turn the far too little, far too late.

Dan Sharp

ABOUT CLAES SUNDIN

Illustrator and author Claes was born in 1957 and lives in the southern part of Sweden. Since finishing four years of studies at the University of Uppsala, he has been active as a teacher, marketer, photographer and art director, among other occupations.

Since childhood, Claes has had a strong interest in everything concerning the combat aircraft of the Second World War and later. This interest stems from the time when he, as a boy of only seven, started building and collecting plastic scale models. Simultaneously, he has been an ardent draftsman for as long as he can remember, as well as an accomplished CGI artist in more recent years. At the present Claes is producing books, writing articles and lecturing. Up to now he has produced over two thousand CGI profiles, mostly of aircraft, but also of Second World War armour.

His previously published books include: Luftwaffe Fighter Aircraft in Profile (1997), Deutsche Jagdflugzeuge (1998), More Luftwaffe Fighter Aircraft in Profile (2002), Luftwaffe Fighter Aircraft, Limited Edition (2011), Luftwaffe Fighter Aircraft, Profile Book No 1 (2013), Allied Fighter Aircraft, Profile Book No 2 (2013), Tiger and Panther Tanks (2014), Luftwaffe Fighter Aircraft, Profile Book No 3 (2014), Luftwaffe Attack Aircraft, Profile Book No 4 (2015), Profiles of German Tanks (2015), Luftwaffe Night Fighters, Profile Book No 5 (2016), Luftwaffe Fighter Aircraft, Profile Book No 6 (2016) and Luftwaffe Bombers, Profile Book No 7 (2017). In addition, he has provided aircraft and tank profiles, photo refinement, and artwork for many other books and papers.

Claes says: "As a long time profile artist, I am well aware that a few of the profiles included in this publication will be the subject of some criticism. The reader however, must acknowledge that all the profiles included are based on solid photographic documentation. I will always use at least one reference photo, more if available, of the subject. I seek the best photos available for the related close-up details as well.

"However, misinterpretations could naturally occur, especially regarding the colours I've chosen for the different profiles. One has to appreciate the difficulty of interpreting the colours from dated black and white photographs. But know that I have, together with my colleagues, made the utmost effort to determine the actual appearance and colouring of the individual aircraft profiles presented here."

LUFTWAFFE BOMBERS — CONTENTS

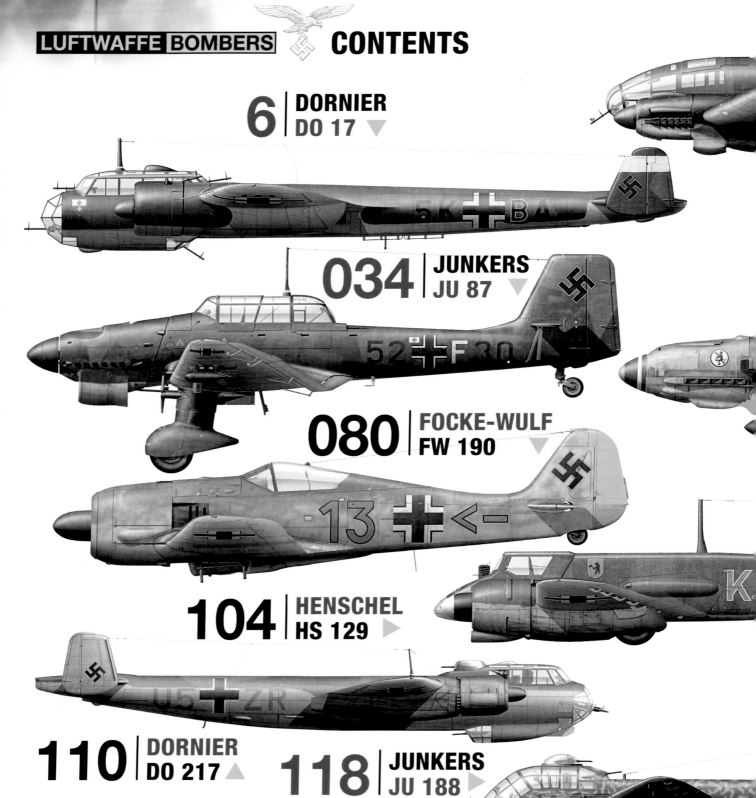

All illustrations:
CLAES SUNDIN

Design:
LUCY CARNELL

Publishing director:
DAN SAVAGE

Publisher:
STEVE O'HARA

Reprographics:
JONATHAN SCHOFIELD & PAUL FINCHAM

Production editor:
DAN SHARP

Marketing manager:
CHARLOTTE PARK

Commercial director:
NIGEL HOLE

Published by:
MORTONS MEDIA GROUP LTD, MEDIA CENTRE, MORTON WAY, HORNCASTLE, LINCOLNSHIRE LN9 6JR.

Tel. 01507 529529

MORTONS MEDIA GROUP LTD

Printed by: **WILLIAM GIBBONS AND SONS, WOLVERHAMPTON**

ISBN: 978-1-911276-75-3

DORNIER DO 17 Z-2 ▲

This aircraft, WNr. 2550, coded 5K+BA, of Stab./KG 3 was hit by flak during a mission south-west of Compiègne, northern France, before being shot down by a pair of Curtiss H-75s of CG 1/5 flown by Captain Jean Accart and Sergeant Francois Morel. The pilot, Hauptmann Georgfriedrich Altvater stationed at Le Culot, Belgium, force-landed it at Redu, France, at 10.15am on May 12, 1940 – two days into the Battle of France.

DORNIER DO 17 Z-2 ▼

Once the French and Belgians had capitulated, the Germans quickly began taking over their airfields in readiness for attacks on Britain. Among the units gather for this purpose was Stab./KG 3, which took up residence at Le Culot, Belgium, in early July, 1940. This aircraft, 5K+EA, is shown in the colours it wore on August 15, 1940 – the day that the unit was ordered to destroy RAF Croydon.

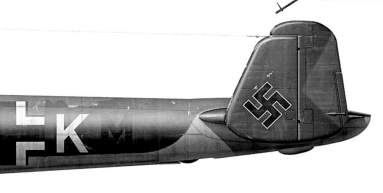

DORNIER DO 17 Z-2 ▲

Stationed at Cormeilles-en-Vexin in France, F1+KM was operated by 4./KG 76. This is how it appeared on August 31, towards the end of the Battle of Britain.

DORNIER DO 17 Z-2 ▼

This bullet-riddled Do 17 Z-2, coded F1+JK, was flown by Unteroffizier Hans Figge of 2./KG 76 on September 15, 1940, when he was attacked by RAF fighters. He managed to evade pursuit but his aircraft was crippled with one engine out. After he crash-landed five miles north of Poix in north-eastern France, his ground crew counted 124 separate bullet impact points on the airframe. Figge and his three aircrew survived.

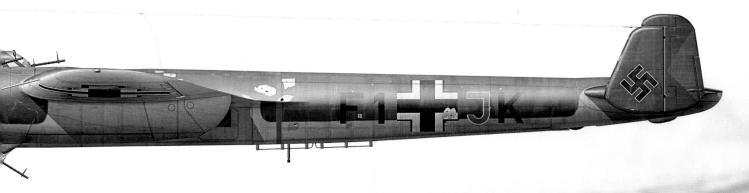

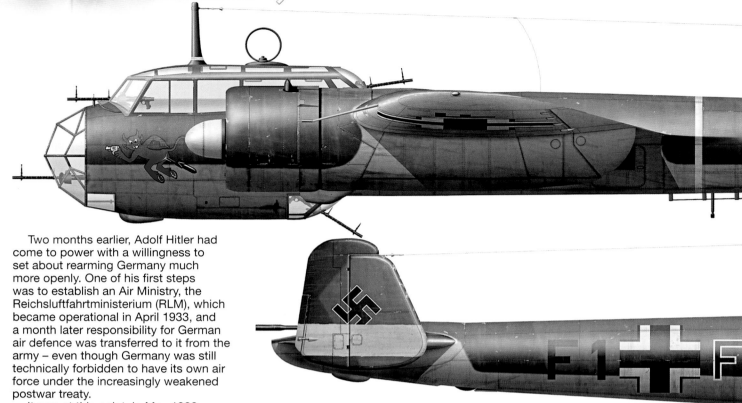

Two months earlier, Adolf Hitler had come to power with a willingness to set about rearming Germany much more openly. One of his first steps was to establish an Air Ministry, the Reichsluftfahrtministerium (RLM), which became operational in April 1933, and a month later responsibility for German air defence was transferred to it from the army – even though Germany was still technically forbidden to have its own air force under the increasingly weakened postwar treaty.

It was at this point, in May 1933, that Dornier received an order for two prototypes of the Do 17 postal aircraft. Events moved quickly and by the end of 1933, the company had been issued with a further contract to develop and supply a high speed cargo aircraft that was capable of carrying bombs.

The Do 17's defensive armament and bomb dropping gear was discussed at a meeting at Dornier on April 13, 1934, and a full wooden mock-up was ready for inspection on May 20, 1934. The original order for two prototypes was increased to three and the first made its maiden flight on November 23, 1934, powered by a pair of BMW VI 7.3 inline engines. The Do 17 V1 was a shoulder-wing all-metal aircraft with a single central tailfin which unfortunately proved insufficient when it came to providing the required level of in-flight stability.

The Do 17 V2, fitted with a twin-fin and rudder arrangement, was ready to fly on May 18, 1935. It had a pair of de-rated BMW VI engines and proved to be an improvement on the single fin layout – resulting in the V1 also being fitted with a twin-fin tail.

The third Do 17 prototype took to the skies on September 19, 1935, and soon defensive weapons testing commenced with various arrangements of machine guns. As production of the various prototypes continued, the aircraft began to acquire a nickname – 'the Flying Pencil' owing to its long thin fuselage. The Do 17 V8 became the prototype for a long-range reconnaissance variant, the

DORNIER DO 17 Z-1 ▽

As the Battle of Britain was drawing to a close in September 1940, 2./KG 77 operated this aircraft, 3Z+LK, from its base in Laon, France.

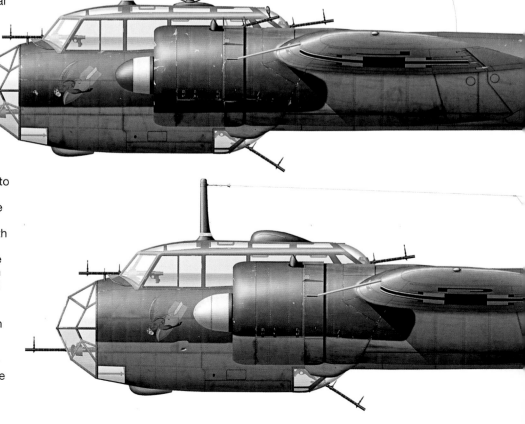

DORNIER DO 17 Z-1 ◄

One of a trio of Do 17s on a mission to bomb London on September 15, 1940, F1+FH, WNr. 2361, flown by Oberleutnant Robert Zehbe of 1./KG 76, was set upon by RAF Hurricanes. Seeing that F1+FH was heading for Buckingham Palace, and having run out of bullets, 504 Squadron Hurricane pilot Ray Holmes rammed it and its tail came off. It crashed into London Victoria station. Zehbe later died of his wounds but Holmes, though injured, bailed out and survived.

DORNIER DO 17 Z-1 ▲

Pilot Rudolf Heitsch of 8./KG 76 crashed his Do 17, F1+FS, in a field at Castle Farm, near Shoreham, in Kent on September 15, 1940. When they reached the wreck, the British were surprised to discover that the aircraft had been fitted with a primitive flamethrower in its tail. A tube, operated by the rear gunner, was linked to oil, nitrogen and hydrogen cylinders. When a fighter began following the bomber, the oil would be dispersed over it, before being set alight. Fortunately for the RAF's pilot, there was too little oxygen at 16,000ft for the device to work – and it only succeeded in covering fighters in oil.

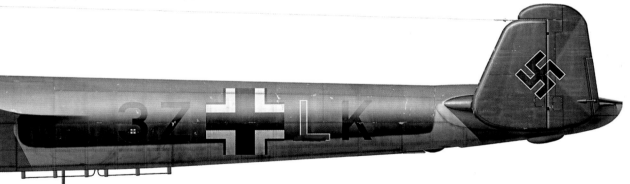

DORNIER DO 17 Z-2 ▼

Despite suffering heavy damage during a mission over Britain, 3Z+JH of 1./KG 77 made it back to the unit's station at Laon, France, during October 1940 before making a wheels-up crash-landing.

THE DO 17 UNDERWENT RAPID DEVELOPMENT DURING THE LATE 1930S, WITH ARMAMENT IN PARTICULAR BEING REGULARLY UPGRADED.

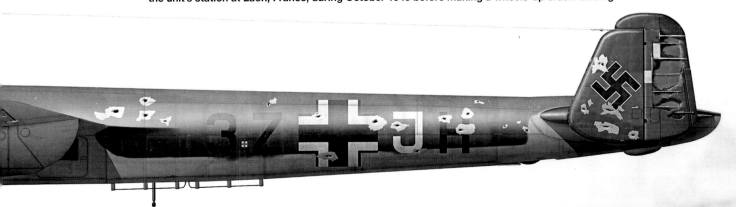

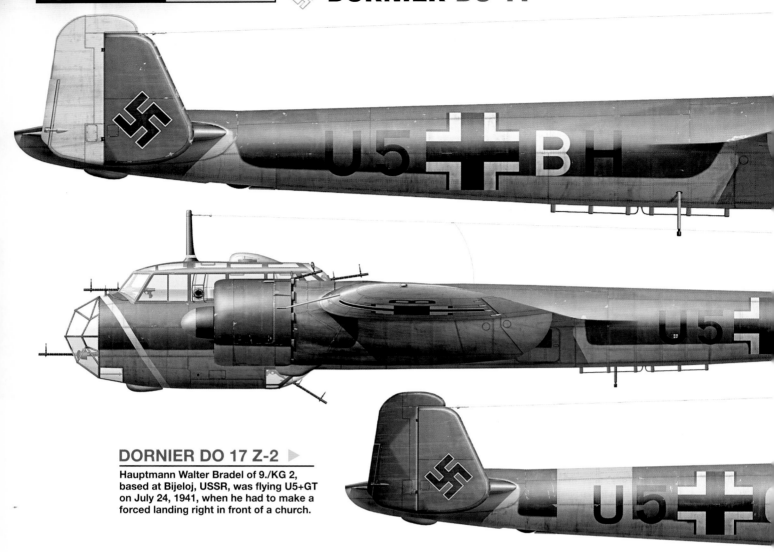

DORNIER DO 17 Z-2 ▶

Hauptmann Walter Bradel of 9./KG 2, based at Bijeloj, USSR, was flying U5+GT on July 24, 1941, when he had to make a forced landing right in front of a church.

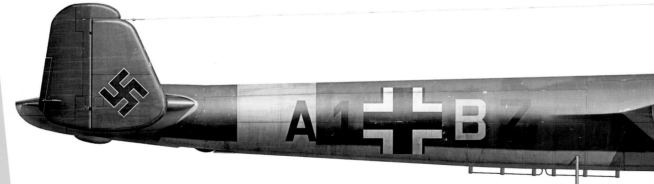

THE SPANISH CIVIL WAR WAS THE IDEAL PROVING GROUND FOR THE DO 17 AHEAD OF ITS OFFICIAL UNVEILING TO THE WORLD

Do 17 F-1, while the V9 was used to test the layout of a high-speed airliner, this still being peacetime.

The Do 17 V15, V16 and V17 were intended as prototypes for the Do 17 E-1 production model bomber and were fitted with Bramo 323 engines, with the V18, V19 and V21 had BMW 132 F engines. Both the Do 17 E-1 and F-1 made their combat debut during the Spanish Civil War in 1937 as part of the Condor Legion, supporting General Francisco Franco's Nationalists.

The Do 17's official international unveiling, however, took place at the Zurich Air Show from July 23 to August 1 that same year. Exhibitors from other countries at the show were astonished and somewhat alarmed when trials demonstrated that the large twin-engine Do 17, in Do 17 M form, was faster than other countries' small fighter aircraft. Also in 1937, the first prototype for the Do 17 P was produced – another reconnaissance variant.

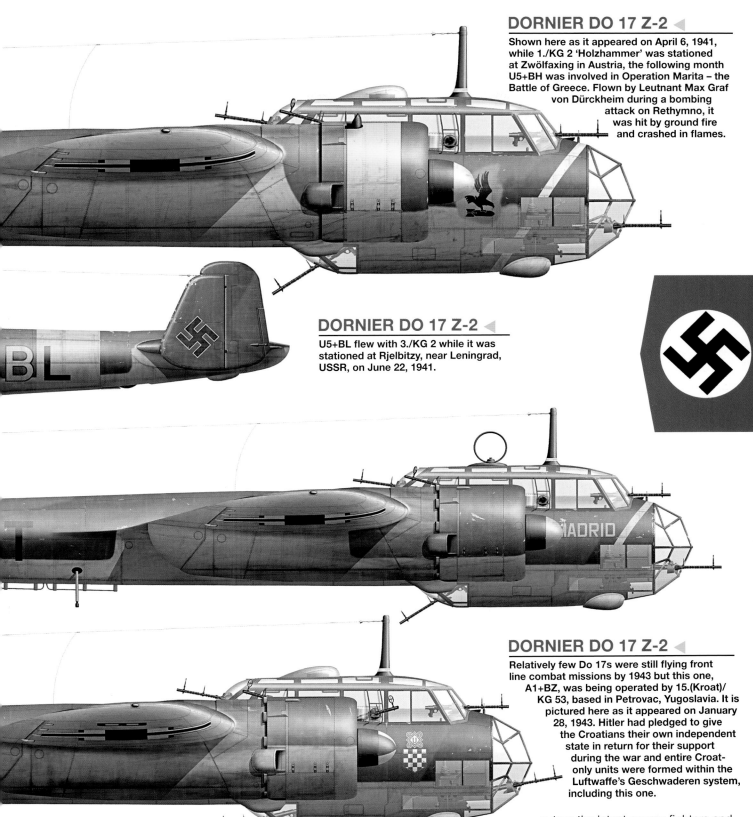

DORNIER DO 17 Z-2 ◄

Shown here as it appeared on April 6, 1941, while 1./KG 2 'Holzhammer' was stationed at Zwölfaxing in Austria, the following month U5+BH was involved in Operation Marita – the Battle of Greece. Flown by Leutnant Max Graf von Dürckheim during a bombing attack on Rethymno, it was hit by ground fire and crashed in flames.

DORNIER DO 17 Z-2 ◄

U5+BL flew with 3./KG 2 while it was stationed at Rjelbitzy, near Leningrad, USSR, on June 22, 1941.

DORNIER DO 17 Z-2 ◄

Relatively few Do 17s were still flying front line combat missions by 1943 but this one, A1+BZ, was being operated by 15.(Kroat)/ KG 53, based in Petrovac, Yugoslavia. It is pictured here as it appeared on January 28, 1943. Hitler had pledged to give the Croatians their own independent state in return for their support during the war and entire Croat-only units were formed within the Luftwaffe's Geschwaderen system, including this one.

However, the best was yet to come. The most successful model in the series was the Do 17 Z. The Z-0 was powered by a pair of 900hp Bramo 323 A-1 engines and had a defensive armament consisting of three MG 15s. The Z-1 increased this to four by adding another in the aircraft's nose. Both of these early variants were considered underpowered, however, and could only manage a bomb load of 500kg. When the new 1000hp BMW 323 P became available for the Do 17 Z-2, payload could be increased to 1000kg and the aircraft could carry up to eight machine guns for defence.

The Luftwaffe was able to field at total of 346 Do 17 Z-1s and Z-2s by December 2, 1939, and by May 11 the following year the total had increased to 422. By now though, the aging Do 17's top speed of 265mph was nowhere near enough to outrun the latest enemy fighters and its defensive armament was far too weak to fight off Spitfires and Hurricanes. During the Battle of Britain, Do 17 units suffered heavy losses.

Those Do 17s that survived were mostly gifted to Germany's allies over the next two years as more advanced bombers such as the Ju 88 and Do 217 became available in large numbers. A small number of Do 17s remained in service with the Luftwaffe until the end of the war, however. ●

HEINKEL HE

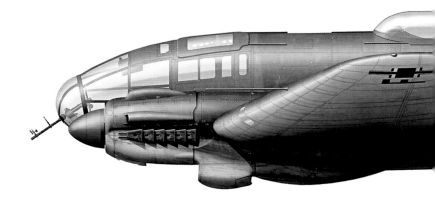

HEINKEL HE 111 P-2 ▼

Kampfgeschwader 27 was stationed at Hannover-Langenhagen, Germany, on May 10, 1940, during the Battle of France. This aircraft, 1G+ML, was part of 3./KG 27.

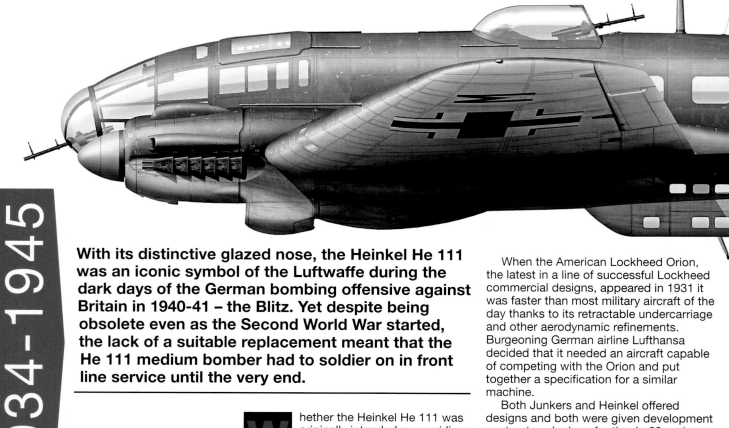

1934-1945

With its distinctive glazed nose, the Heinkel He 111 was an iconic symbol of the Luftwaffe during the dark days of the German bombing offensive against Britain in 1940-41 – the Blitz. Yet despite being obsolete even as the Second World War started, the lack of a suitable replacement meant that the He 111 medium bomber had to soldier on in front line service until the very end.

W hether the Heinkel He 111 was originally intended as an airliner, a bomber, or both might never be known for certain. However, its design certainly followed on from that of the He 70, which was a four-seater passenger aircraft.

When the American Lockheed Orion, the latest in a line of successful Lockheed commercial designs, appeared in 1931 it was faster than most military aircraft of the day thanks to its retractable undercarriage and other aerodynamic refinements. Burgeoning German airline Lufthansa decided that it needed an aircraft capable of competing with the Orion and put together a specification for a similar machine.

Both Junkers and Heinkel offered designs and both were given development contracts – Junkers for the Ju 60 and Heinkel for what would become the He 70. The He 70 V1 first flew in December 1932 and it was clear from the outset that this was going to be a fast machine.

Between March 14 and April 28, 1933,

111

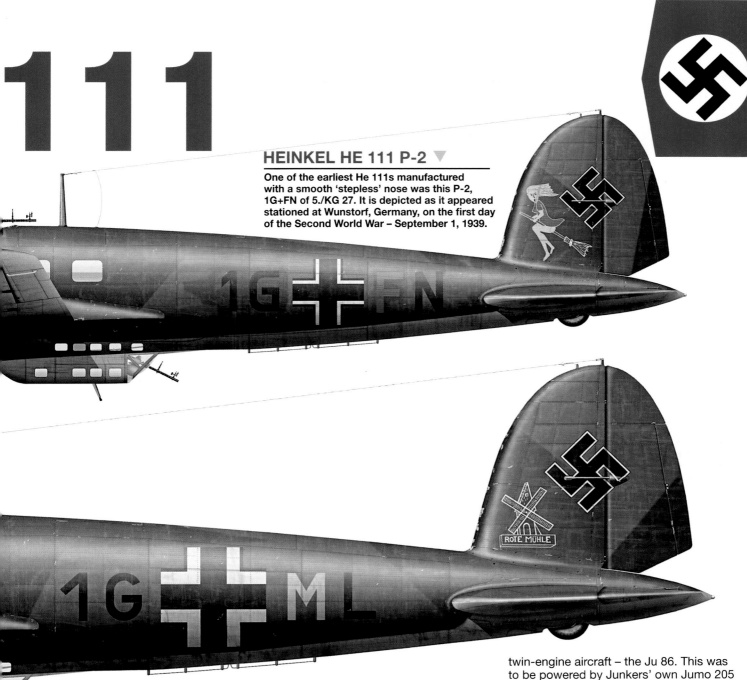

HEINKEL HE 111 P-2 ▼

One of the earliest He 111s manufactured with a smooth 'stepless' nose was this P-2, 1G+FN of 5./KG 27. It is depicted as it appeared stationed at Wunstorf, Germany, on the first day of the Second World War – September 1, 1939.

the He 70 set a series of closed-circuit speed records, and shortly after this seems to have been the point at which the newly formed RLM first expressed an interest in a scaled-up version of the aircraft. It is unclear whether the scaled-up design was instigated by Lufthansa – which certainly wanted a fast twin-engine aircraft capable of carrying up to 10 passengers – the RLM or Heinkel itself.

A development contract was placed and the company's chief designer Siegfried Günter personally led the design of the new twin-engined aircraft. Following a relatively short period of design and approval of a wooden mock-up, He 111 V1 WNr. 713 was constructed at Heinkel Werk Marienehe, Warnemünde. Progress was such that the first test flight was evidently scheduled to take place in

November 1934. In the end, the aircraft was not ready until mid-February and made its first flight on February 24, 1935, with chief test pilot Gerhard Nitschke at the controls. He reported that the He 111 was fast, handled well and had good landing characteristics.

In contrast to the He 70, the He 111 V1 had fabric-covered wings with a 25m span and 92.4sqm area. It was powered by a pair of BMW VI engines – the same powerplant used by the single-engine He 70 – and featured a similar tail arrangement. During later testing, the He 111 V1 was criticised as lacking longitudinal stability when climbing and when being flown at full power. In addition, aileron forces were found to be too strong.

Once again, however, Heinkel found itself competing against Junkers. While work on the He 111 had been ongoing, Junkers had been developing its own

twin-engine aircraft – the Ju 86. This was to be powered by Junkers' own Jumo 205 engine and indeed was ready for its first flight in November 1934. Following early tests, both the Ju 86 V1 and He 111 were sent to the Luftwaffe's Rechlin test centre for comparative evaluation during April 1935. Despite its weaker engines, the He 111 was able to keep pace with the Ju 86 and when both were fitted with the same powerplants the Heinkel design proved to be superior.

Not long after the He 111 V1 had made its first flight, the He 111 V2 was also ready to fly. This was specifically built as an airliner for up to 10 passengers and like the V1 had fabric-covered wings. It also had a reduced wingspan of 23m, with an area of 88.5sqm. Following its first flight on March 12, 1935, it was handed over to Lufthansa as D-ALIX and used for trials. Alongside He 111 V4 D-AHAO and He 111 C D-AXAV it was also used by Kommando Rowehl to secretly take photographs of potential military targets

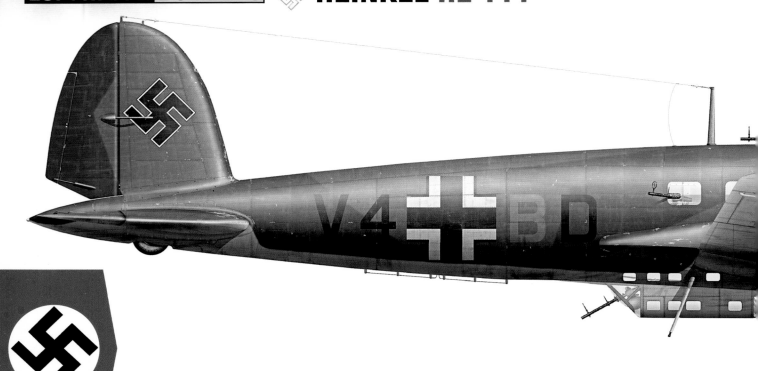

in France, Britain and the Soviet Union during its civilian operations.

The first truly military He 111 was the BMW VI-powered V3, WNr. 714, which also made its maiden flight in March 1935. Wingspan was reduced still further to 22.6m and wing area to 87.6sqm. Despite its intended purpose, it was still given a civilian registration, D-ALES, before being sent to E-Stelle Rechlin during January 1936. It was found that the aircraft could carry a bomb load of 1000kg but this resulted in a severe deterioration of performance. Early trials concentrated on wireless equipment and variable pitch propellers.

For the first four He 111 prototypes, fuselage length remained the same at 17.1m but from V5 onwards it was extended to 17.5m. An initial pre-production run of 15 He 111 A-0s was planned to follow the prototypes but the generally weak performance of the BMW VI prevented this from becoming a reality. Instead, during the summer of 1936 Heinkel began to build seven He 111 B-0s powered by Daimler-Benz DB 600 C engines with variable pitch propellers. This represented a substantial 200hp increase in power from each engine. MG 15 machine gun positions were installed in the nose, upper fuselage and lower fuselage. The lower fuselage position took the form of a retractable cylindrical turret which caused high levels of drag when extended.

An order for 255 aircraft was placed by the RLM and the B-0s were followed by full production B-1s to basically the

HEINKEL HE 111 P-2 ▼

Just five days after this depiction of He 111 P-2 B3+BK at 2./KG 54's station at Werl, Germany, on May 14, 1940, it encountered Hawker Hurricanes over France and was riddled with bullets from end to end. The pilot was forced to make a wheels-up landing between Épinoy and Oisy-le-Verger nine miles south of Douai.

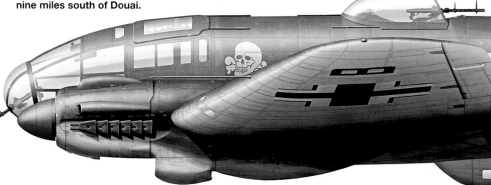

same specification, then the B-2 which had a pair of 950hp DB 600 CGs and the B-3 which was a B-1 modified with special equipment for training new crews. Heinkel's own factories at Rostock and Oranienburg were not up to the task of building so many large aircraft on their own so the work was subcontracted

out to Arado at Brandenburg, Junkers in Dessau, Dornier at Wismar and ATG at Leipzig. The He 111 B had essentially become the Luftwaffe's standard bomber.

FROM B TO E
While the He 111 C was another airliner, the He 111 D was intended as the next

HEINKEL HE 111 H-3 ▼

This H-3, coded V4+BD, was flown by Oberleutnant Gerhard Baecker of Stab III./KG 1, based at Ettinghausen, Germany, on May 13, 1940, during the Battle of France but it is more noteworthy because one of the crew was German aristocrat Prince Heinrich zu Sayn-Wittgenstein – who would go on to become one of the Luftwaffe's most successful night fighter aces, mostly by shooting down British bombers.

HEINKEL HE 111 H-1 ▼

French fighters attacked and shot down this H-1, 9K+AA of Aufklärungs Schwarm I./KG 51, previously of the Stab./KG 51, while it was making a reconnaissance sortie at 3.15pm on May 12, 1940. The unit was based at Lechfeld, Germany, but the pilot of 9K+AA was forced to make a belly-landing at Ferme de Pommard some three miles south-east of Chablis.

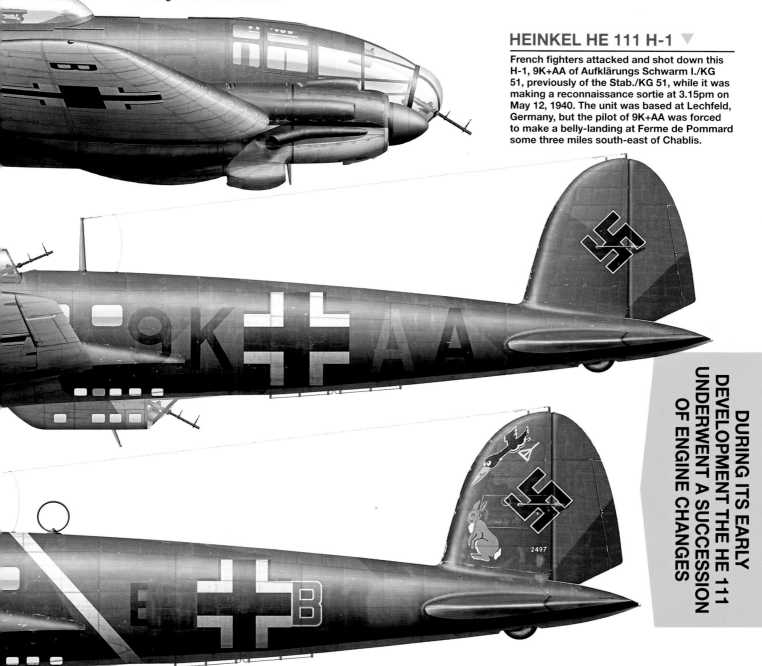

DURING ITS EARLY DEVELOPMENT THE HE 111 UNDERWENT A SUCCESSION OF ENGINE CHANGES

standard production model bomber. It was to be powered by 1047hp DB 600 Ga engines but these were reallocated for use by Messerschmitt, so Heinkel switched to the Jumo 210 G instead. This lacked power however, and the D-1 production series which had begun in 1937 was cancelled after only a few examples had been made. Another new engine was introduced in the form of the Jumo 211 A-1 and this provided the basis for the next major production version of the He 111 – the E series. Work on this variant began with modifications to the He 111 V6, which had the DB 600s it was built with replaced by Jumo 210 Ga units, then early model Jumo 211 A-1s. Early E-0s were then fitted with Jumo 211 A-1s which had retractable radiators and exhaust systems. With an eventual power output of 930hp, the He 111 E-1 was able to carry a bomb load of 2000kg at a top speed of 240mph.

The first He 111 E-1s rolled off the production line in 1938 – just in time to join the Condor Legion fighting in the Spanish Civil War. The E-2 was meant to have improved radio gear but never went into production. The E-3 saw the aircraft fitted with uprated Jumo 211 A-3

HEINKEL HE 111 H-3 ▼

A trio of Blackburn Skua fighters launched from HMS *Ark Royal* at 10.10am on May 15, 1940, intercepted four He 111s over Norway only a few minutes later. These escaped but then a single He 111 of 5./KG 26, was spotted attempting to bomb Allied ships in Narvik's port. The Skuas managed to get five bursts of machine gun fire into it, badly damaging it and forcing pilot Uffz. Siegfried Blume to set down on an iced over lake in Sweden. This went to plan and the four crewmen escaped, beginning the long walk back to their base in Norway, only to be captured by a Polish patrol and sent back to England as POWs. The aircraft, 1H+DN WNr. 6830, survived and was salvaged in 2008.

HEINKEL HE 111 P-2 ▼

Hurricanes shot down B3+BL of 3./KG 54, based at Werl, Germany, on May 27, 1940. The aircraft made a belly landing but was damaged beyond repair.

engines capable of producing 1000hp each. The E-4 had four vertical bomb racks installed within its bomb bay while external bomb racks were installed for the E-5, freeing up space within the fuselage for an additional 835 litre fuel tank, which increased range to 1800km.

The factories producing the He 111 switched to the F series mid-run. This involved a revision of the aircraft's wing planform – from a rounded elliptical shape to straight leading and trailing edges which could be made more quickly and efficiently. The new wing shape had already been trialled using both the V6 and V11 prototypes during 1937.

Twenty-four examples of the standard F-1 were exported to Turkey, while 20 examples of the F-2 with improved radio gear were built for the Luftwaffe. The F-3 was a planned reconnaissance version, the F-4 was a staff communications version and the F-5 was to be similar to the E-5 but was cancelled in favour of yet another new series being started up – the He 111 P.

In the meantime, the DB 600 G-powered He 111 J had been designed specifically at the request of the Kriegsmarine and was capable of carrying both torpedoes and mines. Just 60 (or possibly 90) examples were built and a handful of these survived well into the war as training aircraft or testbeds for guided weapons such as Blohm & Voss's L 10 flying torpedo.

FULLY GLAZED

With the He 111 P series, the type finally appeared in its most distinctive and well-known form. The original 'stepped' cockpit arrangement was replaced with an aerodynamically smooth and fully-glazed cockpit canopy which covered the entire front of the fuselage. Not only that, but the pilot's seat could actually now be raised up to put his eyes level with the upper part of the glazing and a small windscreen panel which gave better visibility for take-offs and landings.

New engines were fitted too – initially the DB 601 Ba, then the DB 601 A-1 – which when combined with the improved aerodynamic form resulted in a top speed increase up to 295mph at an altitude of 16,400ft. While this sounds impressive, it should be noted that with a full bomb load top speed sank right back to a highly disappointing 190mph.

The upper fuselage defensive gun position was now covered by a sliding glass canopy and a streamlined belly gunner position was installed in place of the original which crews had taken to calling the 'dustbin' owing to its shape. In addition, the He 111 P-1 featured a semi-retractable tailwheel to reduce drag.

Forty examples of the He 111 P were built by Junkers at Dessau. In October 1938, the company produced a report that was highly critical of the way in which the aircraft had been designed: "Apparent are the externally poor, less

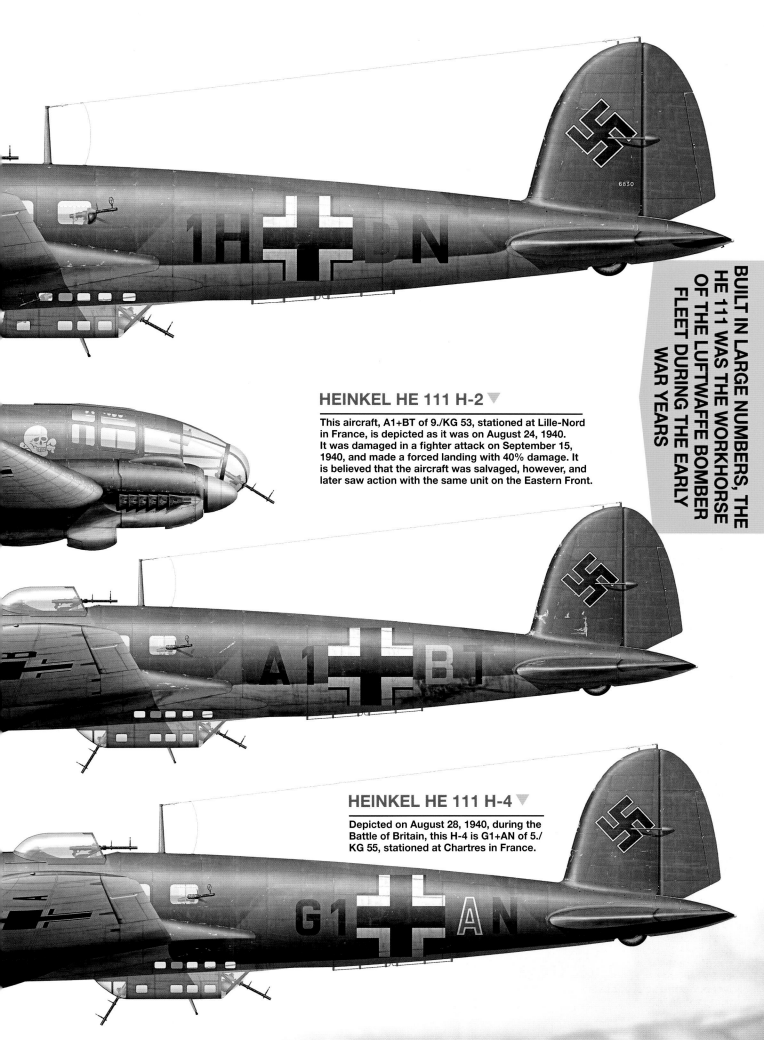

HEINKEL HE 111 H-2 ▼

This aircraft, A1+BT of 9./KG 53, stationed at Lille-Nord in France, is depicted as it was on August 24, 1940. It was damaged in a fighter attack on September 15, 1940, and made a forced landing with 40% damage. It is believed that the aircraft was salvaged, however, and later saw action with the same unit on the Eastern Front.

HEINKEL HE 111 H-4 ▼

Depicted on August 28, 1940, during the Battle of Britain, this H-4 is G1+AN of 5./KG 55, stationed at Chartres in France.

carefully designed components at various locations, especially at the junction between the empennage and the rear fuselage. All parts have an impression of being very weak. The visible flexing in the wing must also be very high. The left and right powerplants are interchangeable. Each motor has an exhaust gas heater on one side, but it is not connected to the fuselage since it is probable that the warm air in the fuselage is not free of carbon monoxide. The fuselage is not subdivided into individual systems, but is attached over its entire length, after completion, to the wing centre section. Outboard of the powerplants, the wings are attached by universal joints. The latter can in no way be satisfactory and have been the cause of several failures."

The P-1 entered squadron service during the spring of 1939 – before the outbreak of the Second World War – and was quickly followed by the P-2 which had stronger armour fitted plus a pair of MG 15s in 'waist gunner' positions on either side of the fuselage. The P-3, of which only eight examples were made, was a training version with dual controls and the option of take-off using the KL-12 catapult.

Next came the P-4, which had the capacity to carry a wide range of different bomb loads and also featured the same five defensive positions as the P-2. The P-5 was another training version, of which around 24 examples were constructed. It was usually unarmed and in some cases even had its bombing gear removed. The P-6 was fitted with the DB 601 N – which was also in great demand for the Messerschmitt Bf 109 E – and as a result relatively few were built. Ten of them were later exported to

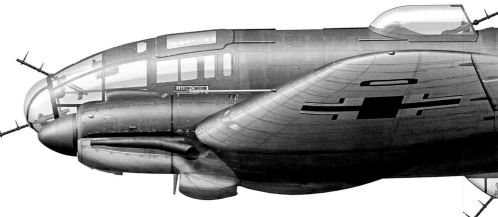

HEINKEL HE 111 H-2 ▲

Having had its port engine disabled by Spitfires then having been hit by ground-fire over England, A1+DA of the Stab./KG 53, based at Lille-Nord, France, made a belly-landing at Old Marsh on the Isle of Grain, Kent, at 5.30pm on September 7, 1940. The aircraft was a total write-off, having been set on fire by the crew.

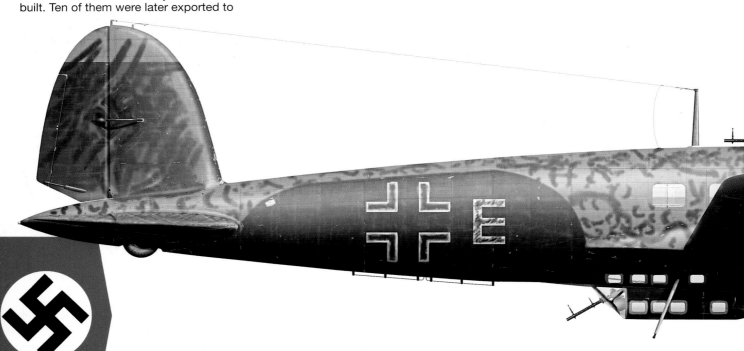

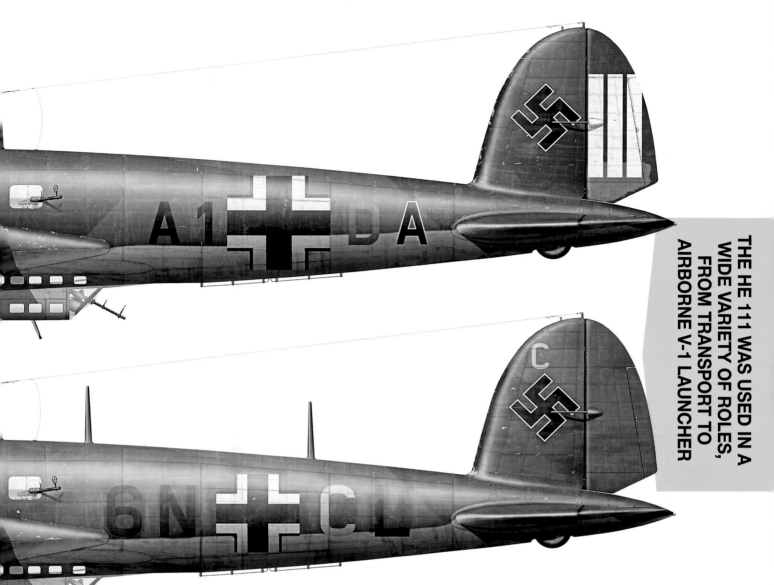

HEINKEL HE 111 H-3 ▲

As a pathfinder, 6N+CL of 3./KGr 100, stationed at Vannes-Meucon, France, was equipped with the X-Verfahren 'Wotan' radio navigation aid. This is how it looked during September 1940.

to Hungary. The He 111 P was the most advanced version of the aircraft on strength with the Luftwaffe on September 1, 1939. Overall, the German air force was operating a total of 705 He 111s at that moment.

THE BIG H

While the He 111 P was in production from 1938 to 1940, Heinkel had not been idle. It was working on the next and, as it would turn out, final major production version of the type – the He 111 H series. This would prove to be by far the most diverse He 111 variant, with numerous different sub-types equipped for dropping torpedoes or launching flying bombs, training new pilots, night time operations, transport duties, pathfinding and high-altitude bombing. Even so, the majority were built as bombers with a host of different engine, armament and equipment variations.

Even as production of the P series got under way, Heinkel was finalising the H's design features. The V17, V18 and V19 prototypes, built as P-1s, were earmarked for H series development work and their flight trials progressed quickly.

The pre-production H-0 series machines began rolling off the production line in June 1939. These were powered by

HEINKEL HE 111

a pair of Jumo 211 A-1s and had self-sealing fuel tanks – a first for the He 111. They were swiftly followed by the full production H-1 which had essentially the same features.

The H-2 was powered by Jumo 211 A-3s but was otherwise the same as the H-1, while the H-3 was powered by 1200hp Jumo 211 D-1s, could carry bombs externally, had five crew instead of four and had a strengthened undercarriage. Defensive armament was increased to five MG 15s and a single MG 17 in the tail. The H-4 was initially fitted with the Jumo 211 D-1 but later this was exchanged for the 211 H-1 or F-1. However, its major modification was an external rack for loads of up to 1800kg – making it capable of carrying and launching torpedoes.

The H-5 was another torpedo bomber but this time had a pair of racks so that up to two torpedoes could be carried at once. Provision was also made within the H-5 for carrying cameras if required an nose armament was upgraded to an MG FF. Auxiliary fuel tanks could be carried in the internal bomb bay to improve range and the undercarriage mainwheels were enlarged to cope with the aircraft's extra weight.

There were a host of detail changes with the H-6 – another torpedo bomber. The radiator installation was altered, the quick-release system for dumping fuel

HEINKEL HE 111 H-6/TROP ▶

Flying a Fairey Fulmar from HMS *Formidable* on May 8, 1941, Robert 'Sam' MacDonald-Hall shot down 1H+AP of 6./KG 26. his Fulmar was hit by return fire, however, and he was forced to crash-land on the deck of *Formidable* after managing to bring the damaged aircraft home.

was modified and some examples had upgraded radio gear. In addition, the H-6 had a pair of the latest Jumo 211 F-1s or F-2s with 1340hp each.

The H-7 was to have been a night bomber with reduced armour plating and several of its machine gun positioned deleted but this was cancelled before it went into production. The next production model in the sequence was the H-8, although this was based on the earlier H-3/H-5 and therefore had Jumo 211

HEINKEL HE 111 H-6 ▼

Camouflaged for the Mediterranean Theatre, 1H+MM flew with 4./KG 26, based at Catania, Sicily, during August 1941.

AS IT BECAME MORE VULNERABLE AS A DAY BOMBER, HE 111S WERE INCREASINGLY SWITCHED TO TORPEDO AND NIGHT BOMBING DUTIES

HEINKEL HE 111 H-6 ▶

This H-6, G1+FT, WNr. 4469 of 9./KG 55, was flown by Lt Mathias Bermadinger, from Kirovograd, USSR, during October 1941. KG 55 had transferred to the USSR from France, having bombed Liverpool, Portsmouth, Birmingham, Coventry, Southampton, London and Manchester during the Blitz. The unit provided support for Army Group South, attacking Ukraine and the Soviet oil fields. In September, KG 55 had supported the Battle of Kiev in which three Soviet armies were destroyed and 600,000 Red Army soldiers captured.

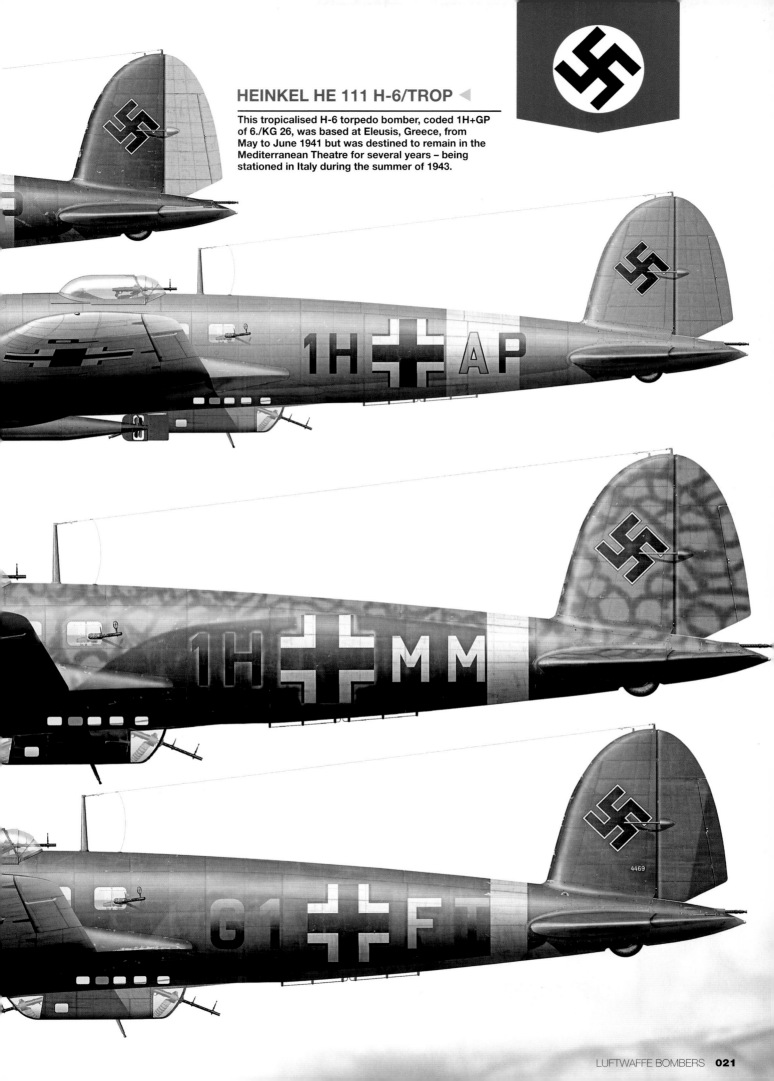

HEINKEL HE 111 H-6/TROP ◀

This tropicalised H-6 torpedo bomber, coded 1H+GP of 6./KG 26, was based at Eleusis, Greece, from May to June 1941 but was destined to remain in the Mediterranean Theatre for several years – being stationed in Italy during the summer of 1943.

HEINKEL HE 111 H-6 ▲

A coat of whitewash was applied to 1G+ER of 2./KG 27, based at Kherson, USSR, as camouflage during the winter of 1941/42. The white was so thin, however, that it weathered very quickly.

D-1s rather than the later more powerful types. Designed as a bomber, the H-8's party piece was a set of barrage balloon cable deflectors. These were heavy, however, so the rear fuselage had to be fitted with a counterweight in order to reset the aircraft's centre of gravity. When it became available, H-8s were retrofitted with Kuto-Nase cable cutters in the leading edge of their wings.

The H-9 is thought to have been essentially the H-1 modified for training purposes with dual controls and a new arrangement of cockpit instruments, although whether it was truly a training version is unclear. Likewise, the H-10 may have been another trainer with most of its defensive weaponry and armour removed, but is believed instead to have been another bomber variant.

The H-11 was an upgraded standard medium bomber based on the earlier H-3. The upper mid turret position was now given a full closable canopy of armoured glass and that position's drum-fed MG 15 was replaced by a belt-fed MG 131. The internal bomb racks could optionally be removed and replaced with additional fuel tanks and an under-fuselage rack could

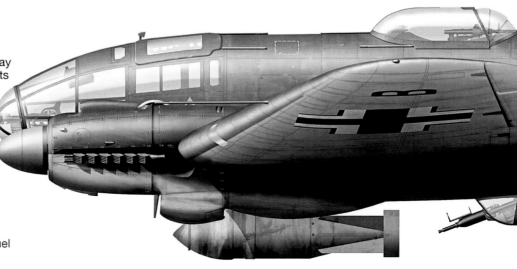

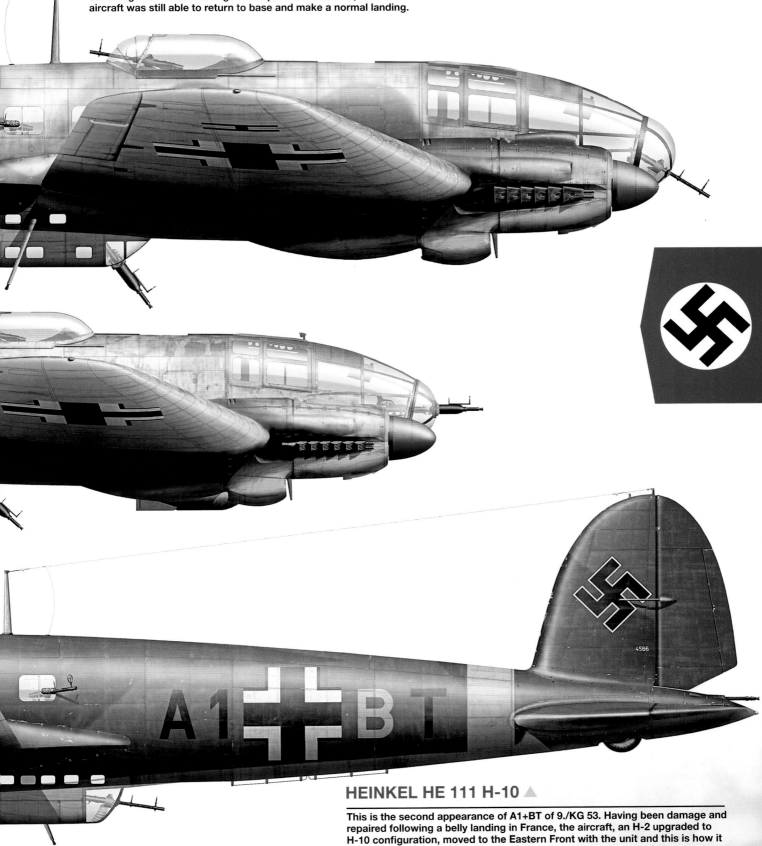

HEINKEL HE 111 H-4 ▼

During a mission in December 1941, this H-4, 1T+HK of 2./KG 28, based at Seshchinskaya, USSR, was rammed by a Soviet Polikarpov I-16 fighter. The 'taran' attack was aimed at the tail section but after striking it a glancing blow, the I-16 rolled over and ploughed into the inner section of the starboard wing tearing out a huge section of fuselage in the process. However, the aircraft was still able to return to base and make a normal landing.

WHILE IT SOON BECAME TOO VULNERABLE TO OPERATE IN THE WEST, THE HE 111 CONTINUED TO SEE SERVICE ON THE EASTERN FRONT

HEINKEL HE 111 H-10 ▲

This is the second appearance of A1+BT of 9./KG 53. Having been damage and repaired following a belly landing in France, the aircraft, an H-2 upgraded to H-10 configuration, moved to the Eastern Front with the unit and this is how it looked when posted at Gostkino, USSR, during September 1942.

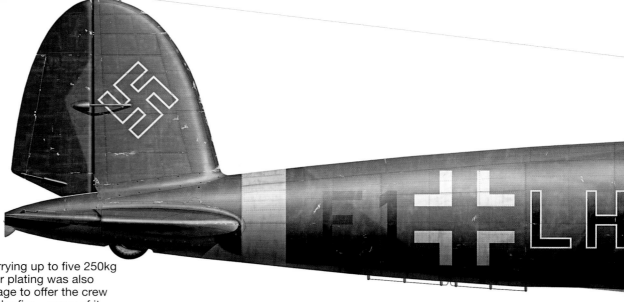

be fitted instead, carrying up to five 250kg bombs. Extra armour plating was also installed in the fuselage to offer the crew better protection under fire – some of it in the lower fuselage where it could be jettisoned to save weight if necessary. The H-11 was the most flexible version of the He 111 to date and some 230 examples had been produced by the summer of 1943.

Fitted with a sophisticated guidance system, the FuG 203 Kehl III transmitter, the H-12 was modified for launching either two Henschel Hs 293 glide bombs or a pair of PC 1400 X 'Fritz X' guided anti-ship bombs from underwing positions. For the first time, the He 111's heating system was also improved with the H-12. Apparently the H-13 designation was simply never applied.

The He 111 H-14 was based on the H-3 but kitted out with a suite of navigation and communications equipment so that it could be used for pathfinder operations. The H-15 is believed to have been another bomber but this is uncertain.

The H-16 was another mass-produced standard bomber in the mould of the H-11. Its armament was usually the same, although in some examples the manned dorsal defensive position was replaced with a DL 131 remote controlled turret. It was powered by a pair of Jumo 211 F-2s and again offered the option of replacing the internal bomb equipment with extra fuel tanks. An unknown number of H-16s were also fitted with the FuG 200 Hohentwiel radar system. A total of 1155 H-16s were manufactured from the end of 1942 to the end of 1943.

The H-17 is thought to have been another trainer, though information on this point is sadly lacking, and the H-18 was a night bomber version of the H-16 with flame dampers fitted to its engines. Side gun positions were removed. The H-19 is believed to have been yet another trainer with dual controls and a modified instrument layout.

By 1944, the He 111 was horrendously outdated and vulnerable to the latest Allied fighters on the Western Front, but

HEINKEL HE 111 H-11 ▼

On November 17, 1942, this H-11 coded 5J+ER of 7./KG 4, stationed at Benina in Libya, was crash-landed in the Western Desert. Unusually, it carried the last two letters of its identification code repeated in small white characters on the leading edge of its port wing.

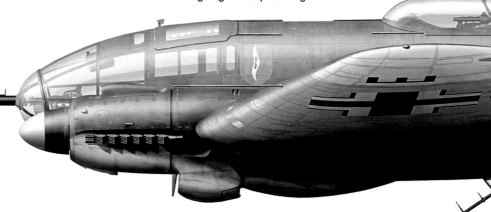

HEINKEL HE 111 H-14Y ▼

A1+AH of 1./KG 53, stationed at Korovye-Selo, USSR, during late December 1942 is depicted with an unusual partial winter camouflage scheme and carrying a 1000kg 'Hermann' bomb. Almost a year earlier, the aircraft had participated in the failed Battle of Moscow but now 1./KG 53 was based nearly 1000km away, close to the Estonian border.

HEINKEL HE 111 H-11 ▼

During late October 1942, 1./KG 76, was based at Armavir in the USSR, carrying out bombing raids against oil targets in Astrakhan and Grozny. F1+LH was an H-11 standard medium bomber and was used intensively. The unit suffered heavy losses and was withdrawn from the Eastern Front the following month.

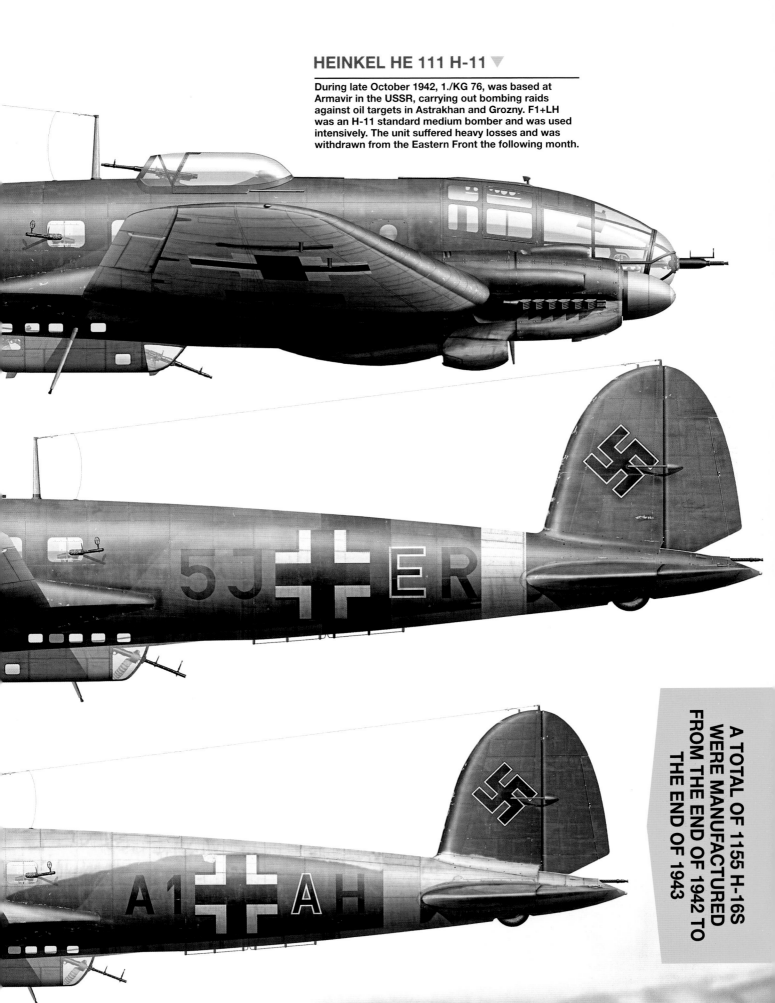

A TOTAL OF 1155 H-16S WERE MANUFACTURED FROM THE END OF 1942 TO THE END OF 1943

it was still useful on the Eastern Front, where opposition remained comparatively light – particularly at higher altitude. The final major production variant of the He 111 was produced during the summer of 1944: the H-20. It had been intended that the H-20 should be fitted with the 1726hp Jumo 213 E-1 but this proved to be too ambitious given the parlous state of German engine production at this stage of the war and most received the standard Jumo 211 F-2 instead.

The H-20 also featured advanced navigational direction-finding gear, Kuto-Nase cutters and the option to fit external bomb racks. It could also be modified to accommodate 16 fully-equipped soldiers or 15 paratroopers. Defensive armament consisted of one MG 131 in the nose, a DL 131/1C turret in the dorsal position, a WL 131/AL or CL in the belly position and one MG 81Z in each side position. The aircraft's tailwheel was enlarged and an

THE HE 111 WAS PRODUCED IN A BEWILDERING NUMBER OF VARIANTS AND SOME DESIGNATIONS APPLIED ONLY TO DRAWING BOARD PROJECTS

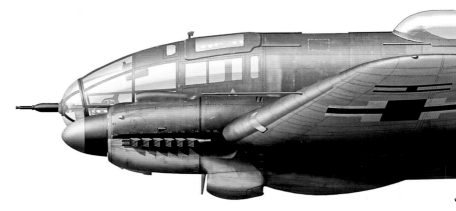

HEINKEL HE 111 H-16/TROP ▼

The Allied invasion of Sicily, codenamed Operation Husky, commenced on the night of July 9/10, 1943, and KG 26, based at Grosseto in Sardina, flew torpedo-bombing missions against the invaders' vessels. Among the aircraft it used was 1H+PH of 1./KG 26.

HEINKEL HE 111 H-16 ▶

The pilot of this aircraft, 6N+AB of Stab I./ KG 100, on July 30, 1943, was Hauptmann Hansgeorg Bätcher. It was his 500th mission and his unit celebrated the achievement on his return to their base at Stalino in the USSR.

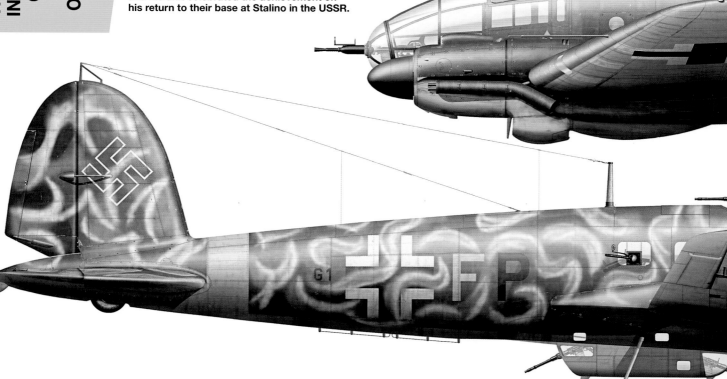

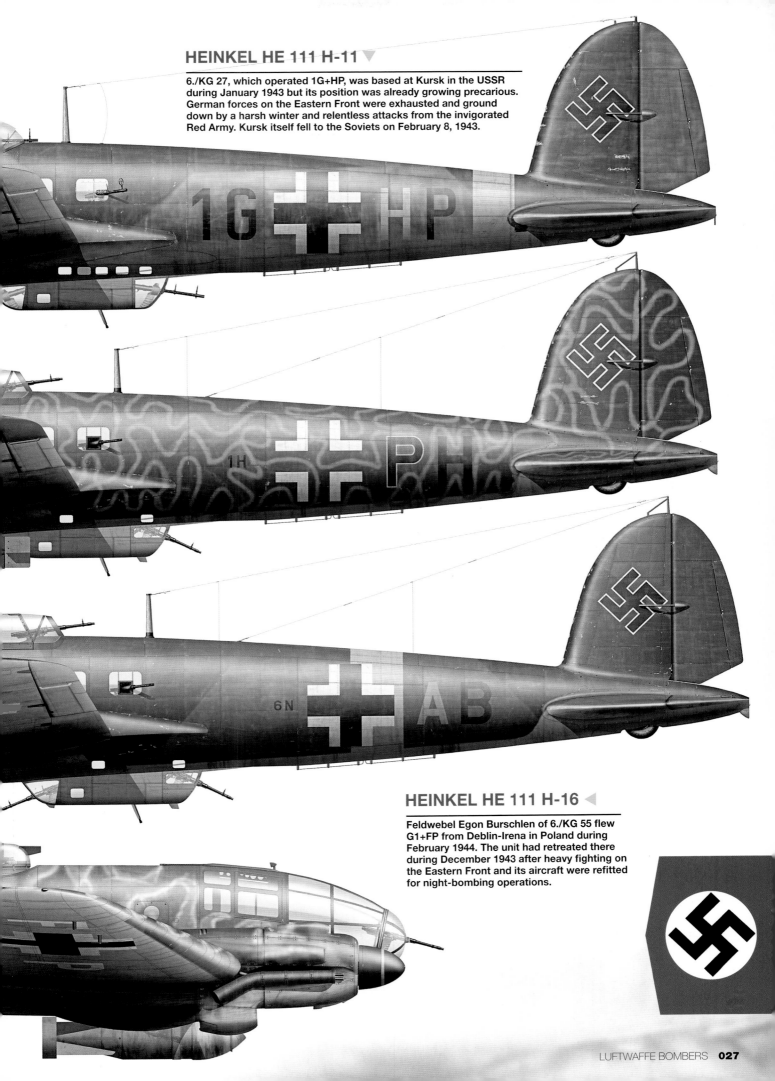

HEINKEL HE 111 H-11 ▼

6./KG 27, which operated 1G+HP, was based at Kursk in the USSR during January 1943 but its position was already growing precarious. German forces on the Eastern Front were exhausted and ground down by a harsh winter and relentless attacks from the invigorated Red Army. Kursk itself fell to the Soviets on February 8, 1943.

HEINKEL HE 111 H-16 ◄

Feldwebel Egon Burschlen of 6./KG 55 flew G1+FP from Deblin-Irena in Poland during February 1944. The unit had retreated there during December 1943 after heavy fighting on the Eastern Front and its aircraft were refitted for night-bombing operations.

optical communications system of signal lamps was installed.

During the summer of 1944 some 550 H-20s were built and 586 H-6s were given upgrades taking them up to H-20 standard.

The H-21 was a high-altitude bomber based on the H-20 but with Hirth TK-9 turbosuperchargers fitted to its Jumo 211 F-2s and the 100 H-22s were built out of existing H-16s and H-20s. These were modified to become the world's first cruise missile launchers – being capable of carrying and launching the Fieseler Fi 103 V-1 flying bomb. Each aircraft could carry just one V-1 on its starboard side, suspended beneath the wing centre section. The H-22 had all of its usual bomb-dropping gear removed and heat protection was added to the tailplane and fin to guard against the hot emissions coming from the V-1 once its engine was fired up.

Finally, the H-23 was the last He 111 variant – apart from projects and the

HEINKEL HE 111 H-20 ▶

Oberleutnant Dietrich Kornblum of 4./KG 53 flew A1+KM from Piastow in Poland, on June 21, 1944. Kornblum, who is generally easily recognisable in photos due to his distinctive round spectacles, had been awarded the Knight's Cross only 12 days earlier. He flew a total of 408 missions during his career and was killed in action on November 28, 1944.

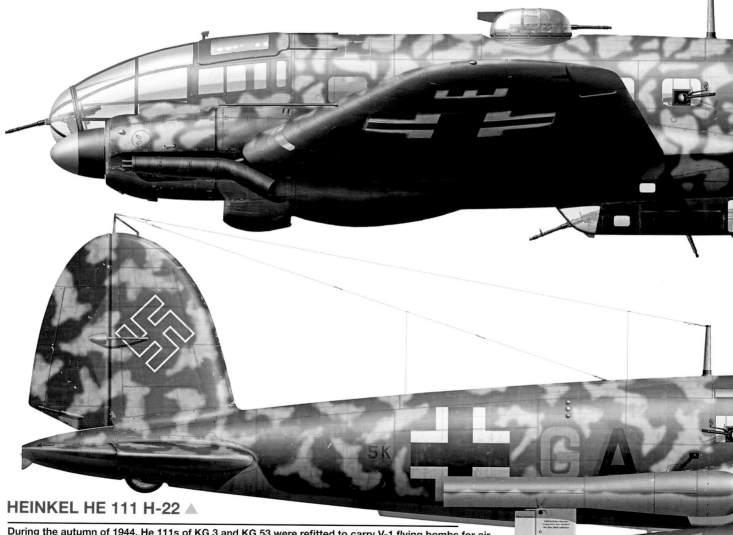

HEINKEL HE 111 H-22 ▲

During the autumn of 1944, He 111s of KG 3 and KG 53 were refitted to carry V-1 flying bombs for air-launched missile attacks against Britain. This example is 5K+GA of the Stab./KG 3, stationed at Bad Zwischenahn, Germany, during November 1944. On Christmas Eve, 1944, at between 5am and 6am a total of 45 V-1s were launched at Manchester from He 111s flying over the North Sea. Just 31 crossed the Yorkshire coast and only seven fell within what is now Greater Manchester. Even so, 42 people were killed in the attack and 109 were injured.

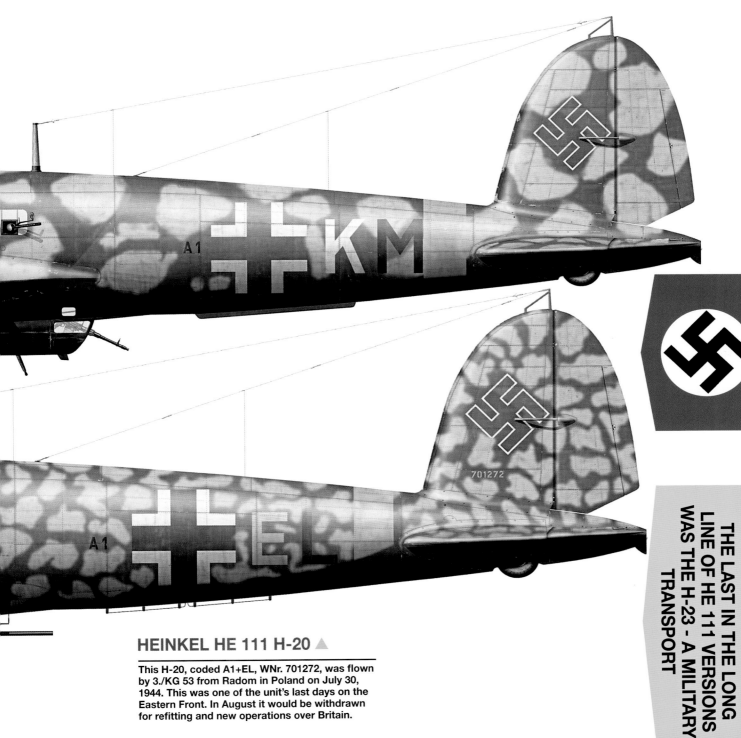

HEINKEL HE 111 H-20 ▲

This H-20, coded A1+EL, WNr. 701272, was flown by 3./KG 53 from Radom in Poland on July 30, 1944. This was one of the unit's last days on the Eastern Front. In August it would be withdrawn for refitting and new operations over Britain.

THE LAST IN THE LONG LINE OF HE 111 VERSIONS WAS THE H-23 - A MILITARY TRANSPORT

outlandish twin-fuselage He 111 Z. The H-23 was a military transport based on the H-20 which could carry up to eight paratroopers or two large containers full of supplies. There were plans to give the H-23 an alternative use as a night bomber but by now the war was entering its final phase and these fell by the wayside. Surviving He 111s saw out the war carrying out a wide range of different tasks – from ferrying supplies to acting as test-beds for experimental equipment, having long since ceased to be viable as front line bombers. ●

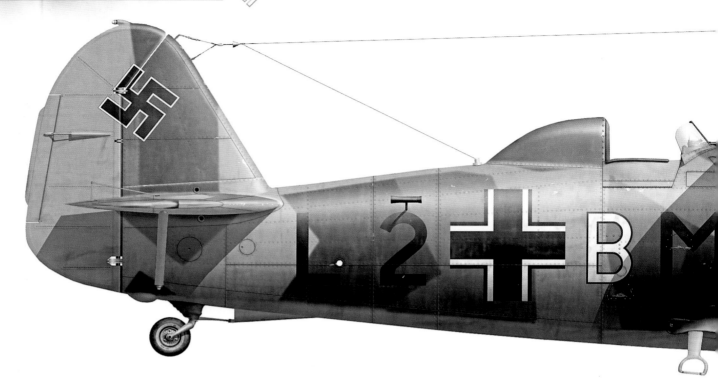

HENSCHEL
HS 123

Just 266 examples of Henschel's single-seat close-support and dive-bomber biplane were built but the type proved so effective that it remained in service until there were simply no more spares and serviceable airframes available.

F ollowing Hitler's rise to power, military planners within Germany worked quickly to draw up new strategies based on his vision of a greatly expanded Luftwaffe. At this stage they foresaw that the most imminent threat to Germany would come from enemy ground forces, so planning for the future air force began to centre on close-support operations.

By the end of 1933, two sets of requirements for new dive-bombers had been drawn up. One was for a robust rapid-availability type which would represent only a modest improvement on existing aircraft and

which could also double-up as a fighter if necessary. The other would make use of new technology to create a much more advanced and specialised dive-bomber in the longer term.

Henschel and Fieseler both tendered for the first requirement – Henschel with what would receive the Reichsluftfahrtministerium designation Hs 123 and Fieseler with what would become the Fi 98. The competition based on the second requirement would be more hotly contested and would ultimately produce the Junkers Ju 87, detailed in the next chapter.

In comparing project proposals there

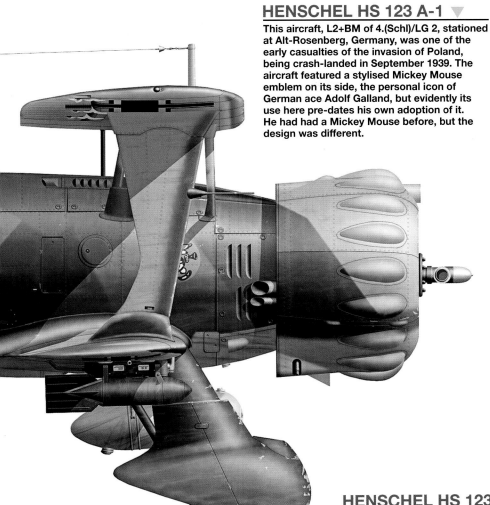

HENSCHEL HS 123 A-1 ▼

This aircraft, L2+BM of 4.(Schl)/LG 2, stationed at Alt-Rosenberg, Germany, was one of the early casualties of the invasion of Poland, being crash-landed in September 1939. The aircraft featured a stylised Mickey Mouse emblem on its side, the personal icon of German ace Adolf Galland, but evidently its use here pre-dates his own adoption of it. He had had a Mickey Mouse before, but the design was different.

was little to choose between the Hs 123 and the Fi 98; both were powered by the specified 715hp BMW 132 A engine and both were deemed capable of carrying the necessary load of four 50kg bombs. Therefore, three prototypes of each were ordered. Detailed design work on the Hs 123 began in February 1934 with completion of a wooden mock-up four months later. Once this was approved, construction work began on the first prototype.

Finished on April 1, 1935, the unarmed Hs 123 V1 was a sesquiplane featuring a sturdy wide-track fixed undercarriage, nearly all-metal construction, wings braced with only a single strut each and a conventional tail unit. It commenced a programme of factory test flights in April, although the precise date of its first flight is unclear, and was first shown in public on May 8, 1935. The Fi 98 V1 is believed to have been completed at around the same time and both were sent to the Luftwaffe's Rechlin test centre for trials.

Despite being powered by the same engine, the Fi 98 proved to be less capable. Its old-fashioned multi-strut wing with wire bracing, narrower undercarriage and unusual double tailplane arrangement

HENSCHEL HS 123 A-1 ▼

Polish Campaign, the type was found to be so effective that the unit was moved west to participate in the Battle of France during 1940. Black 12, pictured here as it appeared on May 21, 1940, was involved in the defeat of a British counterattack at Arras.

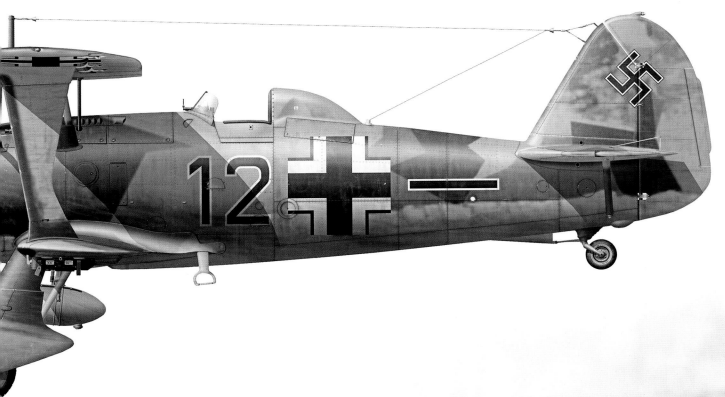

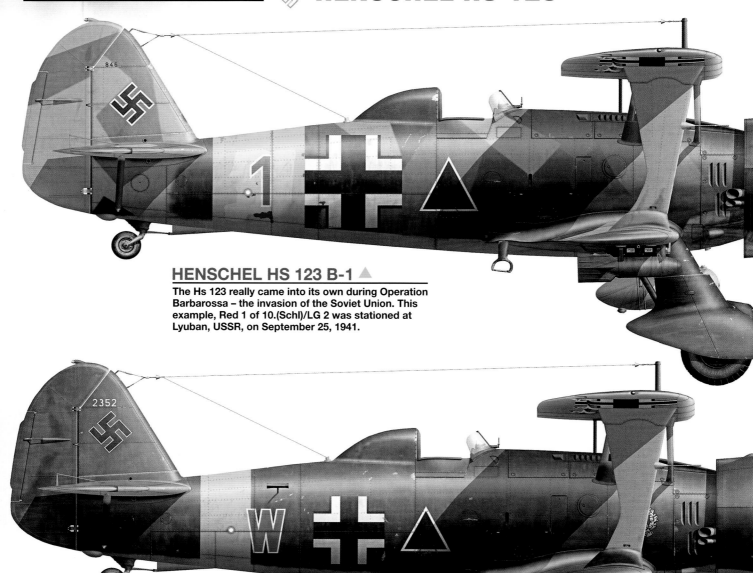

HENSCHEL HS 123 B-1 ▲

The Hs 123 really came into its own during Operation Barbarossa – the invasion of the Soviet Union. This example, Red 1 of 10.(Schl)/LG 2 was stationed at Lyuban, USSR, on September 25, 1941.

THE HS 123 LOOKED OLD FASHIONED BUT OFFERED RUGGED RELIABILITY AND PRECISION IN DIVE-BOMBING

all counted against it and a limited production order was placed for the Hs 123, while the second and third prototypes of the Fi 98 were cancelled.

The second and third Hs 123s were completed just a month after the first. The V2 was fitted with an American-made Wright Cylone GR-1820-F52 engine, which produced 770hp beneath a tight streamlined NACA cowling while the V3 had the same BMW engine as the V1 and was used for bombing trials. Hs 123 was the first to be fitted with a pair of MG 17 machine guns mounted above the engine in the fuselage, firing through the propeller.

Once Henschel had been awarded a production contract for the Hs 123, a fourth prototype was commissioned to act as a pattern machine for the pre-production A-0 series. This took longer than the others to build and was still not ready by January 1936 when the full Hs 123 production order was confirmed. When the V4 was finally finished in mid-April 1936, after the usual

company tests, it was flown to Rechlin for trials involving 10 bomb containers mounted vertically within its fuselage. Each had a single SC 10 bomb inside, which meant that the exterior of the aircraft remained aerodynamically clean. However, it proved extremely difficult to drop a payload this way and accessing the containers on the ground was very difficult. Instead, it was decided that the Hs 123 should carry four SC 50 bombs externally, two under each lower wing, when carrying out its dive-bombing close-support missions.

The A-0 pre-production series ran to 16 machines, with the first examples constructed during May 1936. While this work was ongoing, production lines for the A-1 were being established at Henschel and at AGO Flugzeugwerke in Oschersleben. Soon the lines were running in parallel and the first 'standard' A-1 was ready in September

1936 – before the A-0 series had been completed. By December 1936, more than 20 A-1s and 15 A-0s had been built, with the 16th A-0 being finished in January 1937.

In April 1937, the V3 was destroyed in a crash. While recovering from a dive, a strut connecting the fuselage to the upper wing broke and the upper wing came off. All Hs 123s produced up to this point had to undergo modifications to improve the structural strength of this key area.

Later that year, a number of Hs 123s were built to B-1 standard – the only difference compared to the A-1 being the replacement of fabric sections on the wings and ailerons with metal skin. Plans were laid for an Hs 123 C series, with an enclosed cockpit and a pair of MG 17 machine guns under the lower wings, and Hs 123 V6 was used to test these features, but it never entered production.

Of the 266 Hs 123s built overall, 129 were constructed by AGO. In front line service, the Hs 123 often carried a centreline drop tank due to its limited range using only its internal tank.

However, its rugged construction also meant that it could land and take off from very rough and ready airstrips. It is said that crews could determine whether a field was suitable for the Hs 123 based on whether a car could be driven over it at 50km/h.

Several of the Hs 123's prototypes joined the Condor Legion, fighting in Spain during the Spanish Civil War, while the rest would eventually see action during the Polish campaign of 1939 and the Battle of France in 1940, before seeing out their service careers on the Eastern Front following the invasion of the Soviet Union. ●

HENSCHEL HS 123 B-1 ▲

Black Chevron was flown by Staffelführer Leutnant Josef 'Bazi' Menapace of Stab 7./Schl.G 1 while stationed at Tusov, USSR, on August 8, 1942. Bazi was the first member of his unit to be awarded the Knight's Cross, having completed a total of 650 operational missions. He was eventually killed, on October 6, 1943, when his Fw 190 was shot down by anti-aircraft fire over the Pinsk marshes near Kiev. He was 23.

HENSCHEL HS 123 B-1 ◄

Black Triangle was flown by 2./Schl.G 1, based at Pitomnik-Stalingrad, USSR, during November 1942. Hs 123s flew close-support operations throughout the battle. However, by the end of November the survivors of the German Sixth Army within the ruined city had become surrounded by Soviet forces.

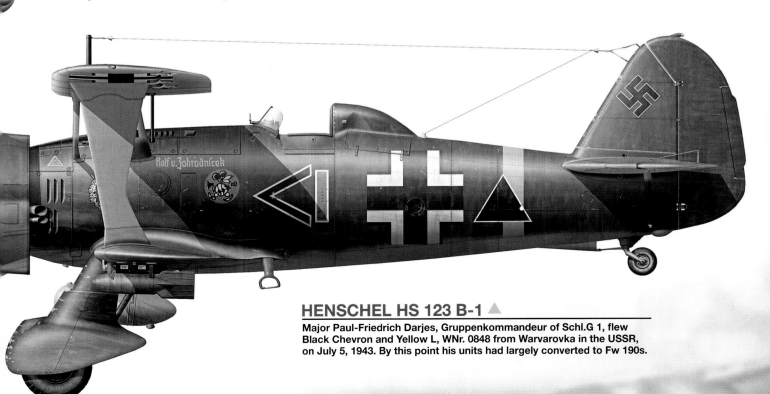

HENSCHEL HS 123 B-1 ▲

Major Paul-Friedrich Darjes, Gruppenkommandeur of Schl.G 1, flew Black Chevron and Yellow L, WNr. 0848 from Warvarovka in the USSR, on July 5, 1943. By this point his units had largely converted to Fw 190s.

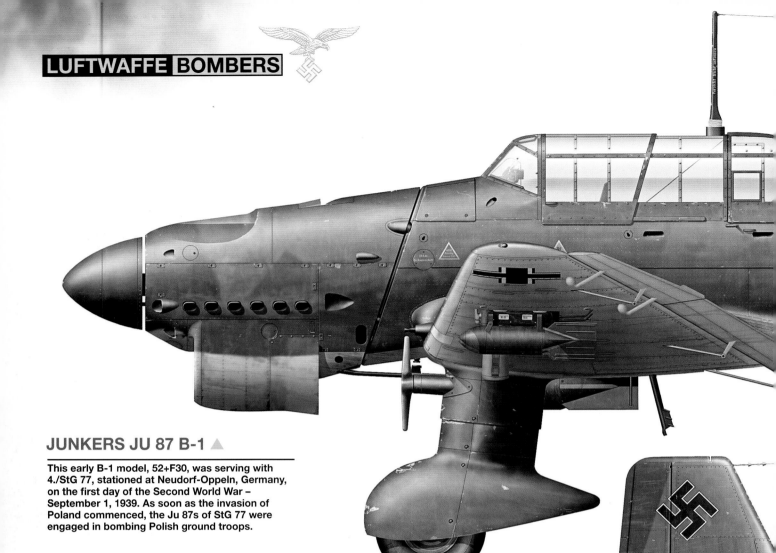

JUNKERS JU 87 B-1 ▲

This early B-1 model, 52+F30, was serving with 4./StG 77, stationed at Neudorf-Oppeln, Germany, on the first day of the Second World War – September 1, 1939. As soon as the invasion of Poland commenced, the Ju 87s of StG 77 were engaged in bombing Polish ground troops.

1935-1945

JUNKERS JU 87

With its inverted gullwings, fixed undercarriage and sirens which screamed as it dived onto its targets, the Junkers Ju 87 was like nothing else when it first saw combat with the Condor Legion in 1937. As the war dragged on, the Ju 87 became the ubiquitous Eastern Front close combat support aircraft.

JUNKERS JU 87 B-1 ▼

Like StG 77, StG 76 was at the forefront during the invasion of Poland in September. German forces made rapid progress and F1+FM of 1./StG 76 is depicted here as it appeared operating out of Kruszyna in Poland during September 1939.

T he decision to base Germany's military strategy on the increasing likelihood of a limited primarily ground-war conflict would have far-reaching ramifications for the Luftwaffe.

The Henschel Hs 123 was chosen to become an 'interim' dive-bomber while a competition was held to find a longer-term advanced dive-bomber, a Sturzkampfflugzeug or 'Stuka' for short. The latter requirement had been drawn up by the end of 1933 and tenders were received from four companies – Arado, Heinkel, Blohm & Voss and Junkers.

Arado put forward its Ar 81, Heinkel the He 118 and Junkers the Ju 87. The Ju 87 had been designed by Junkers engineer Hermann Pohlmann, who had the basic arrangement and layout of the aircraft ready by February 1934. Such was the importance of the competition that all three companies were given development contracts and set to work on building wooden mock-ups of their designs. At the same time a fourth company, the newly established Hamburger Flugzeugbau, also set to work on an aircraft intended to meet the specification, even though it had not been formally invited to tender.

The Ju 87 mock-up, featuring the characteristic inverted gullwing but with a tail configuration consisting of twin fins and rudders was ready by mid-1935 and subjected to formal inspection by RLM representatives on August 7. However, work on the Ju 87 V1 had already begun at AB Flygindustri in Sweden – the incomplete airframe being transported into Germany in late 1934. It was to be powered by a Rolls-Royce Kestrel, 10 examples of which had been ordered by Junkers on April 19, 1934. Its first flight had been scheduled for April 1935 – prior to the official mock-up inspection – but construction difficulties meant that this was delayed until September 17, 1935.

Meanwhile, Hamburger Flugzeugbau's design, the Ha 137, had been able to skip the mock-up stage since it was not an official entrant and went directly to prototype production. As a result the Ha 137 V1's first flight was in April 1935 – well ahead of any of the official entrants. The designs put forward by Arado and Heinkel followed the official process and both, along with Junkers, received an order for three prototypes in August 1935.

Looking remarkably like the Junkers design, the Ar 81 V1 featured a fixed undercarriage, a two-seater cockpit that was open to the rear, and twin fin and rudder tail. It was powered by a Jumo 210 Ca, which was more powerful than the Kestrel, but it was also a biplane – strongly hinting at the fate that was soon to befall it. The DB 600 C-powered He 118 embodied all the very latest ideas about aircraft design. It was a monoplane with a retractable undercarriage, a fully enclosed cockpit and an aerodynamic form evidently based on that of the He 70, just as the design of the He 111 had been.

The Ju 87 V1 stood halfway between the two. While it had a fixed undercarriage and a twin-fin tail, it was also a monoplane and had a fully enclosed cockpit. The Ha 137 had an inverted gullwing like the Ju 87, a fixed undercarriage, a single fin tail and an open single-seater cockpit. And while the first prototypes for the others were being built, the Ha 137 V1 was being test-fitted with a radial Pratt & Whitney Hornet radial engine. The V2 was also completed

with a Hornet engine in May 1935 and both were sent for testing at the Luftwaffe experimental station at Travemünde. This demonstrated that Hamburger Flugzeugbau had done enough to gain entry to the competition and was now also awarded a contract for three prototypes – although it was specified that the V3 should be powered by the inline Jumo 210 since the wide diameter of the Hornet was resulting in reduced visibility from the cockpit.

By the beginning of 1936, Hamburger Flugzeugbau was busy working on its Ha 137 V3, while each of the other companies had now completed their V1s and begun test flights. It was during these early trials, on January 24, 1936, that the Ju 87 V1 crashed with the death of both the pilot, Willy Neuenhofen, and his engineer Heinrich Kreft. An investigation determined that the fault lay with the twin-tail layout, which had proven too weak for dive-bombing. The Junkers Ju 87 V2 was therefore completed with

JUNKERS JU 87 B-1 ◀

Ahead of the Battle of Dunkirk, which preceded the Dunkirk evacuation, Stukas such as S2+MK of 2./StG 77, stationed at Aachen in Germany, operated at the limit of their range against pockets of resistance bypassed by the rapid German advance. This is S2+MK as it appeared on May 14, 1940, ahead of the Battle of Dunkirk. On August 18, 1940, piloted by Leutnant Hans Sinn during an attack on Thorney Island aerodrome, it was shot down by the Hurricane of Pilot Officer C K Gray. Sinn piloted to safety but his gunner, Josef Schmitt, jumped 100ft from the ground without opening his chute and was killed.

JUNKERS JU 87 R-2 ▼

On May 25, 1940, the day before the beginning of the evacuation of British troops at Dunkirk, T6+AM of 4./StG 2, stationed at Cambrai, France, was bombing positions held by the beleaguered French and British forces.

JUNKERS JU 87 R-1 ▲

After being attacked by Gloster Gladiators of 263 Squadron, A5+IL of 3./StG 1, based at Hattjefjelldal, Norway, crash landed at Abisko, Sweden, on June 20, 1940. The crew, pilot Feldwebel Hans Ott and the radio operator/gunner Sonderführer Gunther Brack survived and were interned by the Swedes.

a single tailfin. In addition, the second prototype was strengthened with extra plating and riveted brackets for additional rigidity. Hydraulic dive brakes were also added.

It had been intended that the Ju 87 V2 would be powered by a DB 600 but this was unavailable and after the interim installation of a BMW engine, the V2 finally received a Jumo 210 in March 1936.

THE COMPETITION

A formal series of comparative tests involving all four types now took place during the spring and summer of 1936, with the He 118 being the front runner from the outset and the Ar 81 the least favoured.

Now it became clear that although the Ju 87 retained some outmoded features, such as its fixed undercarriage, its designers had gone to great lengths to ensure that it would be easy to use, practical, rugged and above all reliable – particularly when subjected to the extreme stresses and strains of performing the high-speed dive so essential to dive-bombing operations.

This attention to detail began inside

JUNKERS JU 87

JUNKERS JU 87 B-1 ▶

Twenty-six Stukas of II./StG 51 attacked Portland harbour on the south coast of England at 8.15am on July 4, 1940. Among the vessels assembled there was HMS *Foylebank* – which had been sent to protect the harbour. Unable to take evasive action, the *Foylebank* was attacked again and again, with 22 bombs hitting it. Only one of its guns, a four-incher crewed by Jack Foreman Mantle, was able to fire back. Despite injuries that would prove fatal he managed to get off 55 rounds, shooting down one Ju 87. Among the attackers was 6G+AT of 9./StG 51, based at Norrent-Fontes, France. Mantle received a posthumous Victoria Cross for his heroism.

JUNKERS JU 87 B-1 ▶

Hauptmann Alfons 'Ali' Orthofer of Stab II./StG 77, stationed at Picauville, France, during August 1940 became a minor celebrity in Germany after his Ju 87 S2+AC, painted with a ferocious shark mouth, appeared in the glossy German military magazine Signal. Orthofer was killed on the Eastern Front on October 12, 1942.

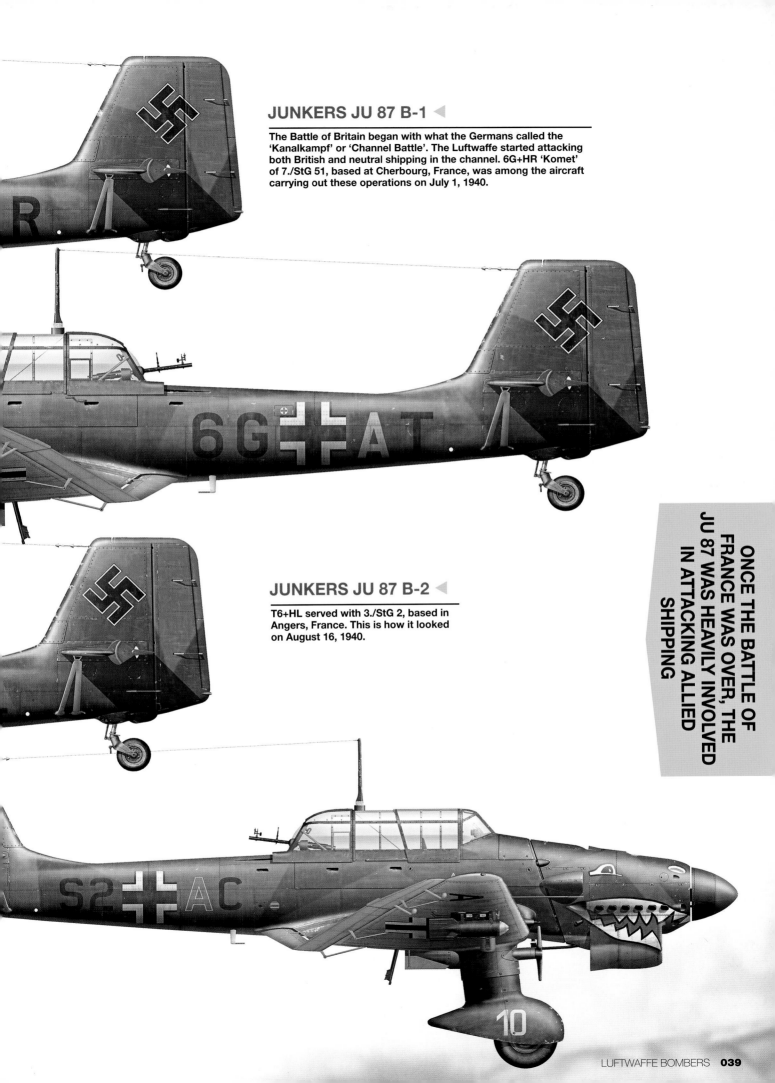

JUNKERS JU 87 B-1 ◄

The Battle of Britain began with what the Germans called the 'Kanalkampf' or 'Channel Battle'. The Luftwaffe started attacking both British and neutral shipping in the channel. 6G+HR 'Komet' of 7./StG 51, based at Cherbourg, France, was among the aircraft carrying out these operations on July 1, 1940.

JUNKERS JU 87 B-2 ◄

T6+HL served with 3./StG 2, based in Angers, France. This is how it looked on August 16, 1940.

ONCE THE BATTLE OF FRANCE WAS OVER, THE JU 87 WAS HEAVILY INVOLVED IN ATTACKING ALLIED SHIPPING

JUNKERS JU 87

JUNKERS JU 87 R-2 TROP ▲

This tropicalised R-2, T6+AC, was flown by Major Walter Enneccerus of Stab II./StG 2, stationed at El Agheila in Libya during March 1941. He had been one of the first Stuka pilots to receive the Knight's Cross on July 21, 1940. In January 1941, he had taken part in the sinking of the HMS *Southampton*. The vessel had been attacked by Enneccerus and 11 other Stukas and was hit by two bombs which caused a devastating fire. Eighty-one men were killed, including many who had become trapped below decks.

the cockpit. Junkers had conducted tests at the mock-up stage to ensure that all of the key instruments required to pilot the aircraft effectively fell easily to hand. All of the key instruments were likewise positioned so as to be easily visible during operations. While the canopy glass was specially arranged to avoid any optical distortions, a small window was also included between the pilot's feet to provide additional downwards visibility – although in practice this would typically end up covered over with oil and grime.

Externally, the Ju 87 was specifically designed to allow easy access to vital components. Hydraulic and electrical systems could be easily accessed for maintenance and even the bomb racks were positioned in a way that would most easily allow technicians to fix or remove them. The fuselage of the aircraft itself was built in two halves – upper and lower rather than left and right – each consisting of four longitudinal stringers and the associated vertical frames. These halves were then bound together by stressed skin sheeting, resulting in an airframe that could withstand immense loads when diving. The wing centre section was made as a single piece and securely bolted onto the lower half of the fuselage, with the outer wings then being added on either side.

JUNKERS JU 87 R-2 ▲

During the final days of the Battle of Greece, in May 1941, S1+MH of 1./StG 3, was stationed at Argos in occupied Greece. Ju 87s had been instrumental in attacking Allied shipping during the battle.

JUNKERS JU 87 R-2 ▶

Long-range R-2s, including S1+AK of 2./StG 3, carried out missions across the Mediterranean and the north coast of Africa from bases in Greece during June 1941.

The join between inner and outer sections was designed in such a way as to allow the outer wings to be quickly and easily replaced as required.

Testing of the Ju 87 progressed well and it was seen as second favourite, behind the He 118. However, the situation changed on July 27, 1936, when Ernst Udet, head of the RLM's technical office, personally took the He 118 up for a diving test. He began a dive from 13,000ft but part-way down the propeller suddenly broke, the reduction gears being sheared away. The aircraft fell apart and Udet was forced to take to his parachute.

In his autobiography, Stürmisches Leben or 'Stormy Life', Ernst Heinkel provides his own interpretation of the competition and the accident which would put an end to the He 118's brief flying career and guarantee smooth passage for the Ju 87 to full production status: "When the He 118 was to be tested before Udet and the engineers of the Technical Department at Rechlin, its development for mass-production was not entirely complete, thanks to the shortcomings of my technical director, Hertel. Furthermore, the machine was entrusted to one of my pilots, Heinrich, who had proved himself to be a good and reliable man. I did not know, however, that he was averse to power dives and to taking certain risks which were to be expected at that stage.

"For the purposes of comparison, three other machines appeared at Rechlin, in addition to the He 118. Arado had sent a solid biplane of mixed construction, with a fixed undercarriage and double tail unit. The bombs, as far as I can remember, hung uncovered beneath the fuselage. The speed was comparatively low. It was the Arado 81.

"Blohm & Voss had sent an all-metal low-wing monoplane designed by Dr Vogt, also of very stout design with a fixed undercarriage, the Ha 137. Junkers had sent the Ju 87, which had dispensed

JUNKERS JU 87 B-2 ▼

A flak hit on the rear cockpit of T6+JK of 2./StG 2, stationed at Ranhewa, USSR, on October 8, 1941, resulted in the death of gunner Walther Schriftman and 40% damage to the aircraft.

with all streamlined elegance, and whose bombs were also hung beneath the body. All the machines were equipped with dive-brakes which enabled them to be kept pin-pointed on the target.

"The competition between these 'hell divers' was an indescribably dramatic spectacle of ear-splitting noise, which seemed almost unbearable at the time. It heralded, without us being aware of it, the terrible effect on the nerves by the Stukas in the first phase of the Second World War. To increase this effect, a typical Udet invention, the 'Jerico trumpet' siren, was installed to increase the scream. For me,

the whole show was a disappointment, although the choice finally rested between the Junkers 87 and my own machine.

"At the decisive moment, Heinrich faltered before making his power dive. While the Junkers pilot virtually stood on his head, Heinrich did hardly more than a steep dive. The decision to choose the Junkers 87 which, in comparison with the slender He 118, looked like a bumblebee, seemed almost a foregone conclusion.

"Udet, however, came over to me. 'I won't make up my mind at the moment. I must dive your bloody machine myself. I'll come out to Marienehe.' He arranged to pay me a visit on June 27. That day I received a visit from Colonel Lindbergh, who had been in Germany several days, on a tour of inspection of German aviation. I

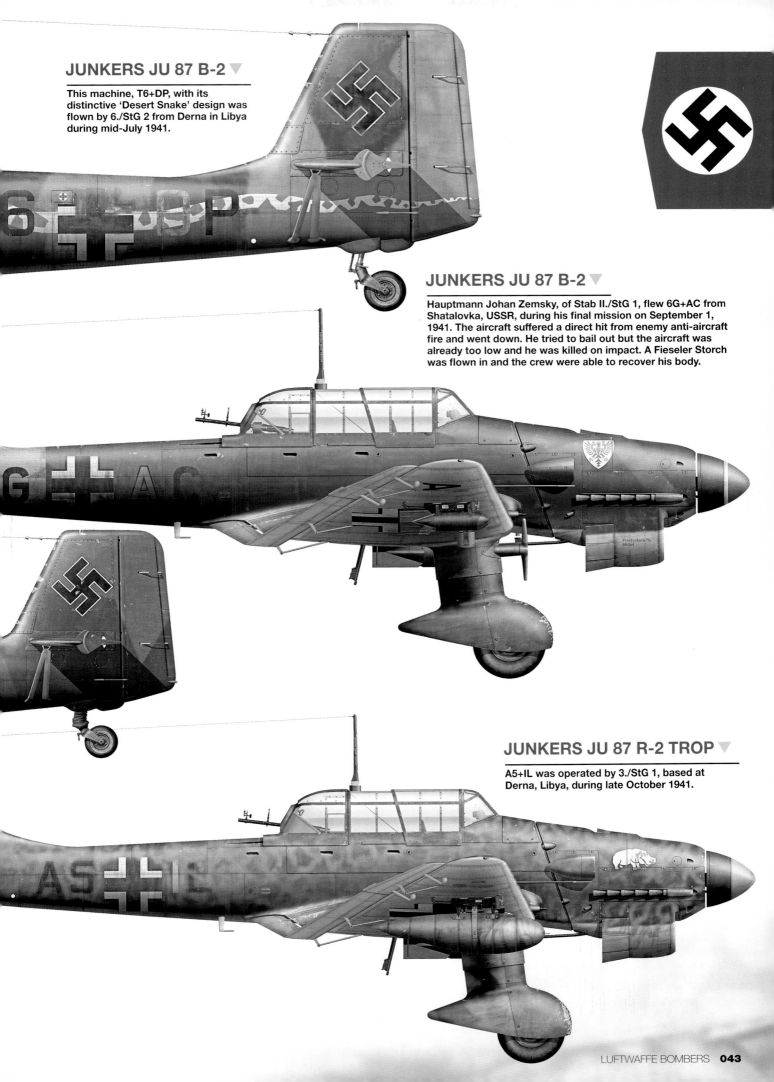

JUNKERS JU 87 B-2 ▼

This machine, T6+DP, with its distinctive 'Desert Snake' design was flown by 6./StG 2 from Derna in Libya during mid-July 1941.

JUNKERS JU 87 B-2 ▼

Hauptmann Johan Zemsky, of Stab II./StG 1, flew 6G+AC from Shatalovka, USSR, during his final mission on September 1, 1941. The aircraft suffered a direct hit from enemy anti-aircraft fire and went down. He tried to bail out but the aircraft was already too low and he was killed on impact. A Fieseler Storch was flown in and the crew were able to recover his body.

JUNKERS JU 87 R-2 TROP ▼

A5+IL was operated by 3./StG 1, based at Derna, Libya, during late October 1941.

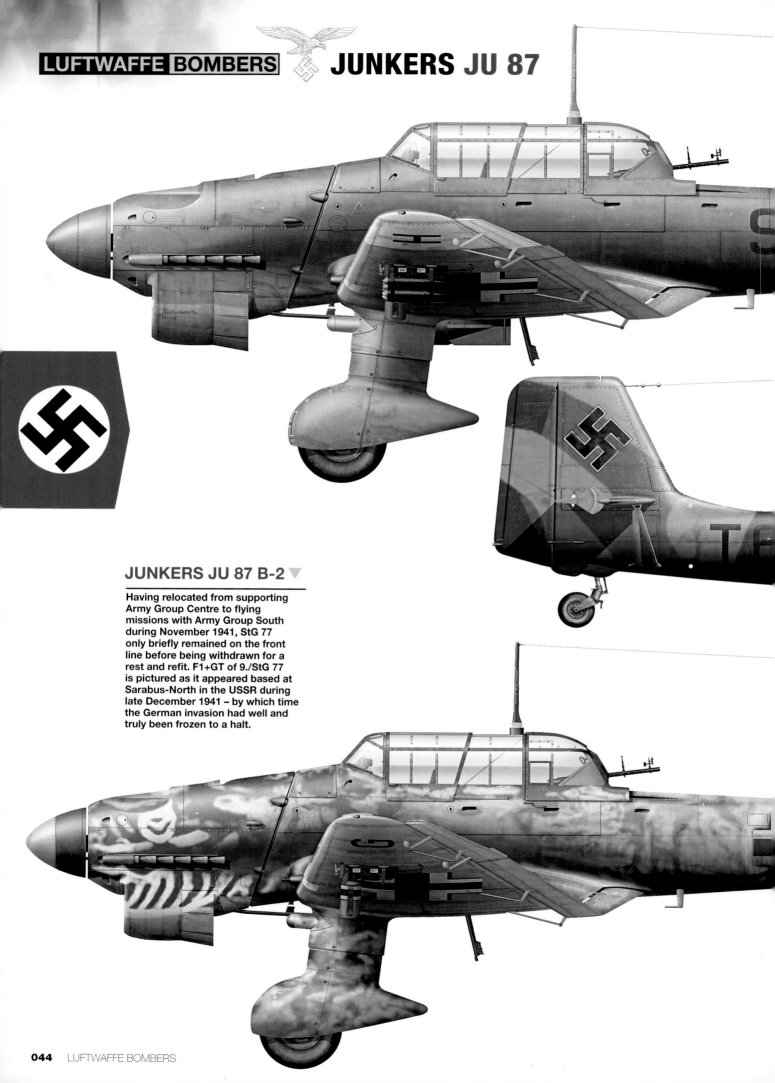

JUNKERS JU 87 B-2 ▼

Having relocated from supporting
Army Group Centre to flying
missions with Army Group South
during November 1941, StG 77
only briefly remained on the front
line before being withdrawn for a
rest and refit. F1+GT of 9./StG 77
is pictured as it appeared based at
Sarabus-North in the USSR during
late December 1941 – by which time
the German invasion had well and
truly been frozen to a halt.

JUNKERS JU 87 B-2 TROP ◄

Having been operated from bases in Greece during the spring, S1+HK of 2./StG 3, was at Derna, Libya, by mid-November 1941.

THE JU 87'S FAMOUS WHEEL SPATS WERE OFTEN REMOVED ON THE EASTERN FRONT AS THEY QUICKLY CLOGGED WITH MUD, DIRT OR SNOW

JUNKERS JU 87 B-2 TROP ▼

While this side of T6+AN of 5./StG 2 'Immelmann', shows only desert camouflage – the other side sported a huge snake decoration. The aircraft is seen here stationed at Bir El Gobi in Libya during December 1941.

"He examined, with the greatest interest, all the types I could show him, particularly the He 70, the 111 and the 118. He scanned the metal machines with an experienced and professional eye. As he had received the same frankness in all the other German factories, in 1936, he probably knew more about the German Luftwaffe than anyone in the whole world. This doubtless came partly from a wish to impress the famous American, but also to let it be seen that there was not the slightest thought of rivalry between the German and American air forces at that time.

"While I tried to answer all his questions in my rusty English, Köhler came up and announced, 'Udet has landed at Marienehe and wants to fly the He 118.' 'Let him fly it, then,' I said. 'I can't get away now, but tell him to look out for the propeller pitch control and that he had better treat the machine with respect.' Köhler disappeared. A few moments later, I drove Lindbergh to Rostock to show him my other factory. As we were wandering among the planes on the third floor, I thought I heard some unusual sound like an engine being revved up by a madman.

"Then there was silence and we went on. A few minutes later, Raphael Thiel caught my arm and tried to pull me aside. I made my excuses to Lindbergh and told Schwärzler to carry on with the visit. 'Udet has crashed with the 118,' Thiel whispered to me. I looked at him in horror. 'Is he dead?' I asked. Thiel shrugged his shoulders. He did not know. He had been telephoned and I was to go to Marienehe at once. I ran off without saying goodbye to Lindbergh and drove off. I found Nitschke, who told me that

received instructions from the RLM to hide nothing from him. Lindbergh landed that morning in Warnemünde accompanied by the American Air Attaché, a tall commander named Mail. I had not met Lindbergh before. He looked older than he really was, despite his chubby face and his hair fluttering boyishly in the wind.

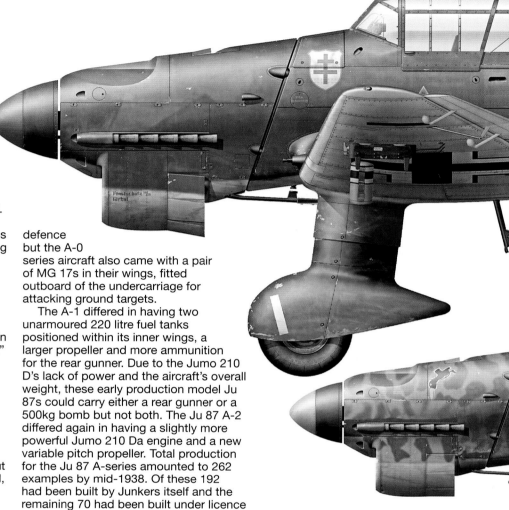

Udet had baled out and had landed in a cornfield. 'He paid no attention to anything,' he said, still out of breath. 'He did not look at the propeller pitch control. The prop and the whole box of tricks came off. The tail broke off and the pieces are lying over there. We saw Udet hanging from the parachute and picked him up. He came to, but only for a moment.' 'Go on – what's happened?' Nitschke knew no more. Udet had only groaned and said that they should let him lie there, as he was finished. Then he swore at our 'bloody death-trap', and had fainted again when he was taken off in the ambulance."

THE WINNER

With the other three machines defeated, a full production order for the Ju 87 was pending but further modifications were still required. In particular, it was felt that the Jumo 210 A was too weak and lacking in power. It had been hoped that the DB 600 would be fitted in its place but this still proved to be unavailable. Instead, the initial series of seven (later increased to 11) Ju 87 A-0s was ordered with the slightly more powerful Jumo 210 D fitted. A new flattened engine cowling was devised for the A-0 series which provided the pilot with better forward visibility and the rear fuselage was lowered to also improved the rear gunner's view. The gunner was armed with an MG 15 for

LIKE MANY GERMAN NON-FIGHTER AIRCRAFT, THE JU 87 INITIALLY SUFFERED FROM HAVING A WEAK ENGINE

defence but the A-0 series aircraft also came with a pair of MG 17s in their wings, fitted outboard of the undercarriage for attacking ground targets.

The A-1 differed in having two unarmoured 220 litre fuel tanks positioned within its inner wings, a larger propeller and more ammunition for the rear gunner. Due to the Jumo 210 D's lack of power and the aircraft's overall weight, these early production model Ju 87s could carry either a rear gunner or a 500kg bomb but not both. The Ju 87 A-2 differed again in having a slightly more powerful Jumo 210 Da engine and a new variable pitch propeller. Total production for the Ju 87 A-series amounted to 262 examples by mid-1938. Of these 192 had been built by Junkers itself and the remaining 70 had been built under licence at Weser Flugzeugbau.

The Ju 87's greatest weakness, its low-powered engine, was finally addressed with the B-series which had been planned and worked on for about a year before a short series of six B-0 aircraft were built during early 1937. These were powered by the Jumo 211 Aa which produced 1000hp – an increase of 280hp compared to the Jumo 210 D. Following hot on their heels came the full production series B-1. This was fitted with the even more powerful Jumo 211 Da with 1184hp.

In order to accommodate the bulky Jumo 211, the Ju 87 had needed a fuselage redesign and Junkers took the opportunity to install a single radio mast in place of the A's twin masts. Perhaps the most visually striking difference was the landing gear: where the Ju 87 A's fixed gear had featured huge aerodynamic fairings, the Ju 87 B's wore only a lightweight pair of spats.

An optional addition to the Ju 87 which became available at this stage was the siren – known today as the 'Jericho trumpet'. This simple siren, effectively a little wooden propeller, was usually fitted to the forward edge of the undercarriage

JUNKERS JU 87 R-2 TROP ▲

Today A5+HL, WNr. 5954, of 3./StG 1 is one of only two complete surviving Ju 87s in the world – preserved at the Museum of Science and Industry in Chicago, Illinois. Back in January 1942, the aircraft was stationed in Libya where it was captured by British forces before being handed over to the Americans.

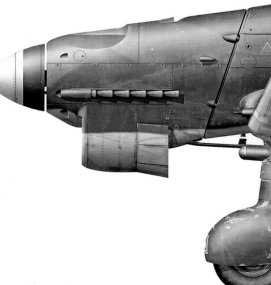

JUNKERS JU 87 R-2 ▼

In the depths of winter, on January 9, 1942, T6+IR of 7./StG 2 was dug in at Rzhev in the USSR.

JUNKERS JU 87 B-2 ▲

F1+AN was flown by the Staffelkapitän of 8./StG 77, Hauptmann Gerhard Bauhaus, while stationed at Sarabus-North in the USSR during February 1942. Bauhaus flew 482 Stuka missions before suffering fatal wounds during an attack near Rostov-on-Don on July 22, 1942. Rostov was captured by German forces three days later.

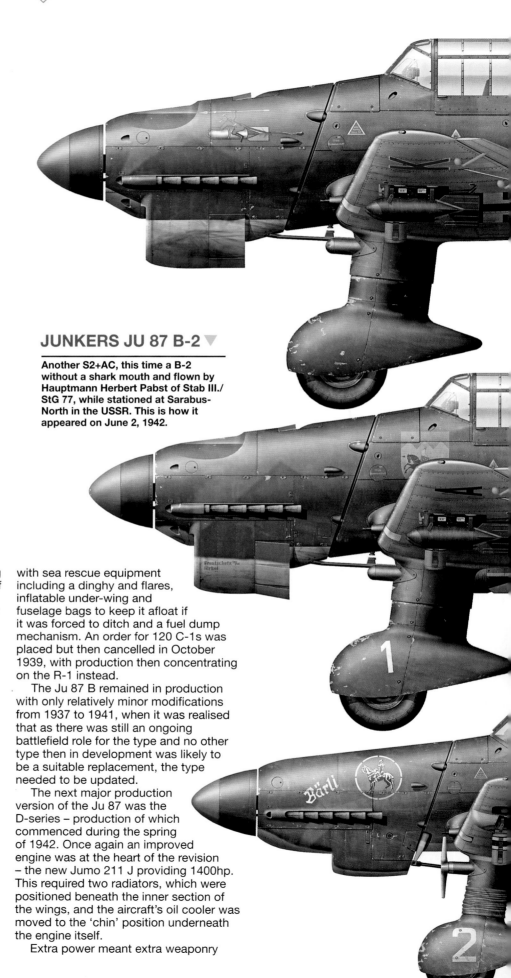

JUNKERS JU 87 B-2 ▼

Another S2+AC, this time a B-2 without a shark mouth and flown by Hauptmann Herbert Pabst of Stab III./ StG 77, while stationed at Sarabus-North in the USSR. This is how it appeared on June 2, 1942.

fairing. It was not an integral part of the B-1's design but could be installed if it was felt that it would have an effect on enemy ground targets during the mission.

The 'trumpet' sound has become so well known that for a time it was regularly used as an audio effect in films whenever an aircraft of any sort entered a steep dive. At the time, however, Stuka pilots disliked having it fitted because it could not be turned off – at least at first – which meant that the crew were forced to listen to it whining even in level flight.

At the beginning of the Second World War, the Luftwaffe was able to field 336 Ju 87 B-1s. The B-2 which followed had cowling flaps which could be closed using an oil hydraulic system. Another version of the Ju 87 B was the Ju 87 R. The out-of-sequence letter 'R' denoted Reichweite or 'range' since this version of the B-series was fitted with internal fuel lines running to the outer wing stations which allowed the fitment of two 300 litre drop tanks. An additional oil tank was also fitted but otherwise the R-series was essentially a Ju 87 B which could carry 600 extra litres of fuel on top of its existing internal tank capacity of 480 litres – more than doubling the aircraft's range. The R-1 had the lower-powered Jumo 211 Aa, while the later R-2 had the Jumo 211 D.

ONGOING UPGRADES

The Ju 87 C was intended to be a specialised naval variant capable of carrying either torpedoes or bombs. Ju 87 V10 and V11 served as prototypes for the variant and the V10 first flew in March 1938 fitted with arrester gear for aircraft carrier landings. While the V10 had the standard B-0 wing the V11, which first flew in May, tested folding wings which would make it better suited to carrier operations.

The C-series was also to be fitted

with sea rescue equipment including a dinghy and flares, inflatable under-wing and fuselage bags to keep it afloat if it was forced to ditch and a fuel dump mechanism. An order for 120 C-1s was placed but then cancelled in October 1939, with production then concentrating on the R-1 instead.

The Ju 87 B remained in production with only relatively minor modifications from 1937 to 1941, when it was realised that as there was still an ongoing battlefield role for the type and no other type then in development was likely to be a suitable replacement, the type needed to be updated.

The next major production version of the Ju 87 was the D-series – production of which commenced during the spring of 1942. Once again an improved engine was at the heart of the revision – the new Jumo 211 J providing 1400hp. This required two radiators, which were positioned beneath the inner section of the wings, and the aircraft's oil cooler was moved to the 'chin' position underneath the engine itself.

Extra power meant extra weaponry

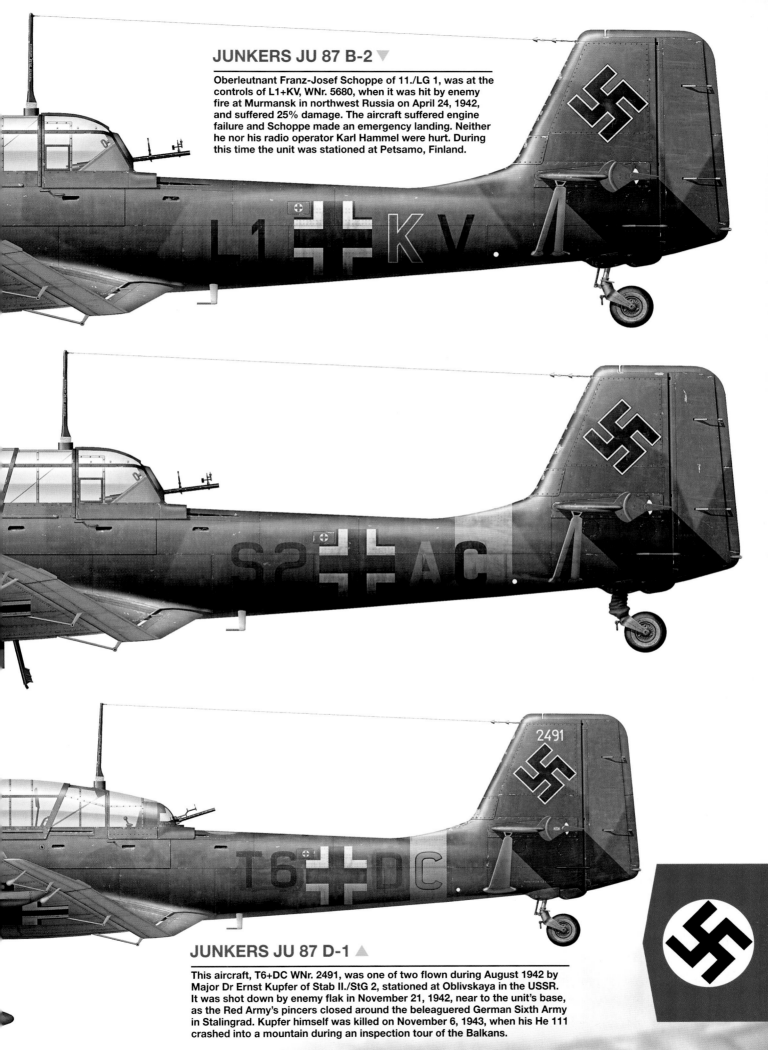

JUNKERS JU 87 B-2 ▼

Oberleutnant Franz-Josef Schoppe of 11./LG 1, was at the controls of L1+KV, WNr. 5680, when it was hit by enemy fire at Murmansk in northwest Russia on April 24, 1942, and suffered 25% damage. The aircraft suffered engine failure and Schoppe made an emergency landing. Neither he nor his radio operator Karl Hammel were hurt. During this time the unit was stationed at Petsamo, Finland.

JUNKERS JU 87 D-1 ▲

This aircraft, T6+DC WNr. 2491, was one of two flown during August 1942 by Major Dr Ernst Kupfer of Stab II./StG 2, stationed at Oblivskaya in the USSR. It was shot down by enemy flak in November 21, 1942, near to the unit's base, as the Red Army's pincers closed around the beleaguered German Sixth Army in Stalingrad. Kupfer himself was killed on November 6, 1943, when his He 111 crashed into a mountain during an inspection tour of the Balkans.

JUNKERS JU 87

THE JU 87 WAS RUGGED AND DEPENDABLE BUT COULD ONLY OPERATE WITH A HEAVY ESCORT LATER IN THE WAR

JUNKERS JU 87 D-1 ▲

Ju 87 D-1 WNr. 2491 was previously coded T6+DC when flown by Major Dr Ernst Kupfer of Stab II./StG 2 but this was subsequently changed to T6+AN. As depicted here, the aircraft was flown by Hauptmann Joachim Langbehn of 5./StG 2, stationed at Karpovka in the USSR during October 1942. While flying another aircraft, T6+DM, on November 25, 1942, Langbehn and his radio operator Josef Laus were shot down by flak following an attack on Perelasovsky. The aircraft burned on impact and both crewmen were killed.

JUNKERS JU 87 D-1 ▶

The commander of StG 3, Oberstleutnant Walter Sigel, flew S7+AA during October 1942 while based on Crete. He was killed as a passenger on board a Fi 156 Storch on May 8, 1944, when the aircraft's pilot Oberleutnant Gerhard Bolz flew into a defensive cable that German forces had stretched across a narrow valley near Trondheim, Norway, to protect the battleship Tirpitz.

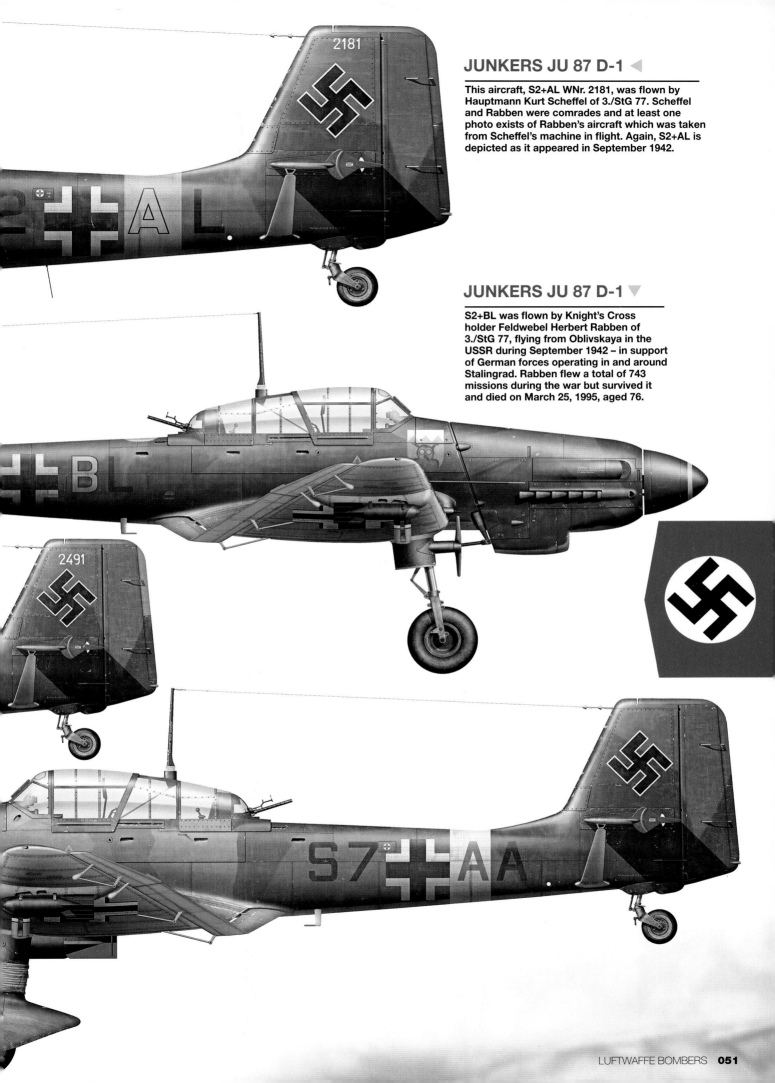

JUNKERS JU 87 D-1 ◄

This aircraft, S2+AL WNr. 2181, was flown by Hauptmann Kurt Scheffel of 3./StG 77. Scheffel and Rabben were comrades and at least one photo exists of Rabben's aircraft which was taken from Scheffel's machine in flight. Again, S2+AL is depicted as it appeared in September 1942.

JUNKERS JU 87 D-1 ▼

S2+BL was flown by Knight's Cross holder Feldwebel Herbert Rabben of 3./StG 77, flying from Oblivskaya in the USSR during September 1942 – in support of German forces operating in and around Stalingrad. Rabben flew a total of 743 missions during the war but survived it and died on March 25, 1995, aged 76.

JUNKERS JU 87

could be carried so the Ju 87's bomb load increased dramatically from the B's 500kg to 1800kg on the D. Internal fuel carrying capacity was also increased to a maximum of 800 litres and the type had the option of drop tanks included as standard.

In addition, the Ju 87 D's cockpit was redesigned to offer the crew greater visibility while also improving the aircraft's overall aerodynamic form. The crew also benefited from greater armour protection and the rear gunner was re-equipped with a twin-barrel MG 81 Z 7.92mm machine gun.

While the D-1 was the standard dive-bomber variant, the D-2 was a tropicalised version with engine filters for harsh operating conditions which also included further armour enhancements. Unfortunately, performance suffered and relatively few D-2s were built. The D-3 included the extra armour without the filters and did go into production. The D-4 was to have been a torpedo carrying version with the addition of two MG 151/20 cannon but it never entered production.

The D-5 offered further significant enhancements to the Ju 87 design as a whole; despite being based on the D-3 it had wings that were 60cm longer and the MG 17 wing guns were replaced with the two MG 151/20s that had been intended for the D-4. The cockpit floor window was strengthened and an extra hinge was added to each aileron for added strength. In this form the aircraft could dive faster and its range was improved too.

From 1942 to mid-1944, a total of some 3300 Ju 87 D-1s, D-2s and D-5s were built.

THE GUSTAV
The last version of the Ju 87 to see action during the Second World War was the G-series – equipped specifically for anti-tank operations. Towards the end of 1942 it was decided that further tankbusters were needed to combat Soviet armour on the Eastern Front and work began on a new development of the Ju 87 D-series.

JUNKERS JU 87 D-3 ▲

Hauptmann Werner Roell of Stab I./StG 77 flew S2+AB while stationed at Kramatorskaya in the USSR during July 1943. Roell had a colourful career as a pilot – switching from flying Ju 52 transport aircraft to dive-bombing with the Ju 87. Then during early 1945 he converted to the Me 262 jet fighter and flew with Adolf Galland's famous Defence of the Reich unit JV 44. He died on May 10, 2008, in Switzerland.

FITTED WITH A PAIR OF 3.7CM CANNON, THE JU 87 G WAS A FORMIDABLE TANK-BUSTER

JUNKERS JU 87 D-3 ▶

This aircraft, S7+JN of 5./StG 3, is depicted as it appeared while based at Argos, Greece, during October 1943.

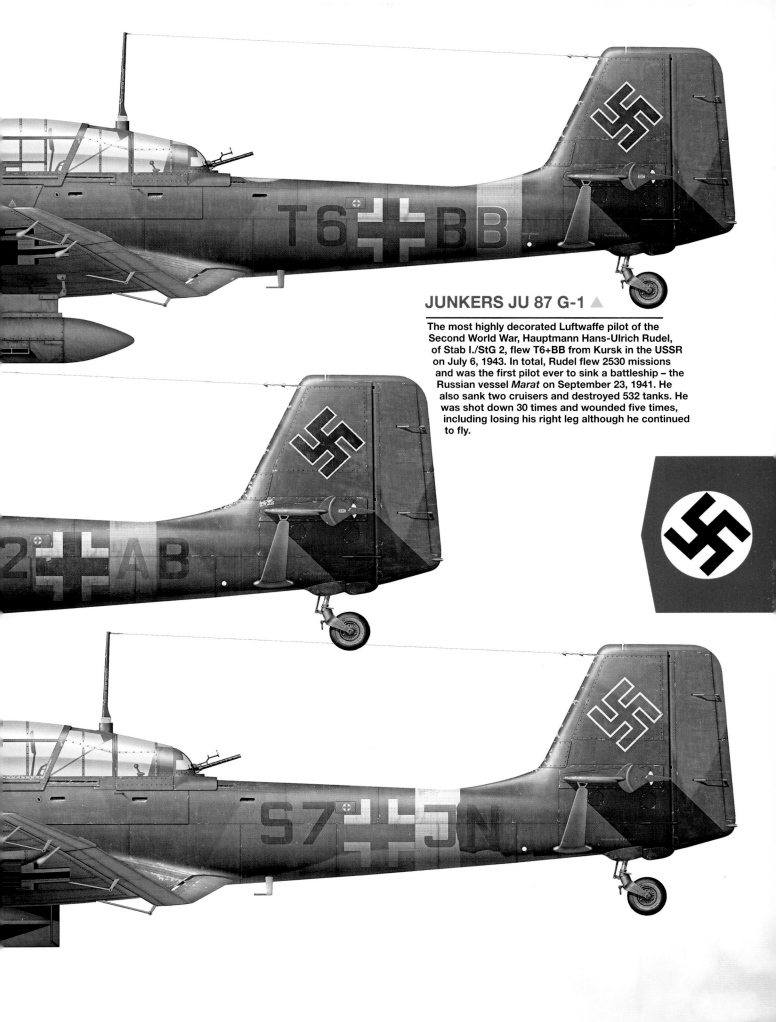

JUNKERS JU 87 G-1 ▲

The most highly decorated Luftwaffe pilot of the Second World War, Hauptmann Hans-Ulrich Rudel, of Stab I./StG 2, flew T6+BB from Kursk in the USSR on July 6, 1943. In total, Rudel flew 2530 missions and was the first pilot ever to sink a battleship – the Russian vessel *Marat* on September 23, 1941. He also sank two cruisers and destroyed 532 tanks. He was shot down 30 times and wounded five times, including losing his right leg although he continued to fly.

JUNKERS JU 87

JUNKERS JU 87 D-5 ▶

S7+AH of 1./SG 3, as it appeared while based at Dorpat, Estonia, February 1944 – fitted with a Stuvi 5B bombsight mounted on its upper windscreen. A few months later, the unit having been moved to Finland, it was being flown by Oberleutnant Hans Törfer. During this period I./SG 3 flew 1200 sorties and dropped a total of 540 tons of bombs in support of Finnish ground forces. A total of 15 Ju 87s were lost along with nine crew missing in action, four wounded and one killed.

JUNKERS JU 87 D-5 ▶

Major Friedrich Lang of Stab III./SG 1 flew A5+AD in dull camouflage for his 1000th combat mission on March 7, 1944, while stationed at Vitebsk in the USSR. Lang had racked up his missions flying Ar 96s and Hs 129s as well as Ju 87s. He ended the war with only eight more missions recorded. During his final sortie on March 13, 1945, he ground looped a Fw 190 F-9 after making it back to base and was hospitalised. He survived the war and died on December 29, 2003.

JUNKERS JU 87 D-3 ▲

6G+AD was flown by Major Otto Ernst of Stab II./SG 1, based at Wesenberg, Estonia, during March 1944.

THE JU 87 D INTRODUCED A MORE STREAMLINED AND SPACIOUS COCKPIT PLUS IMPROVED INTERNAL FUEL CAPACITY

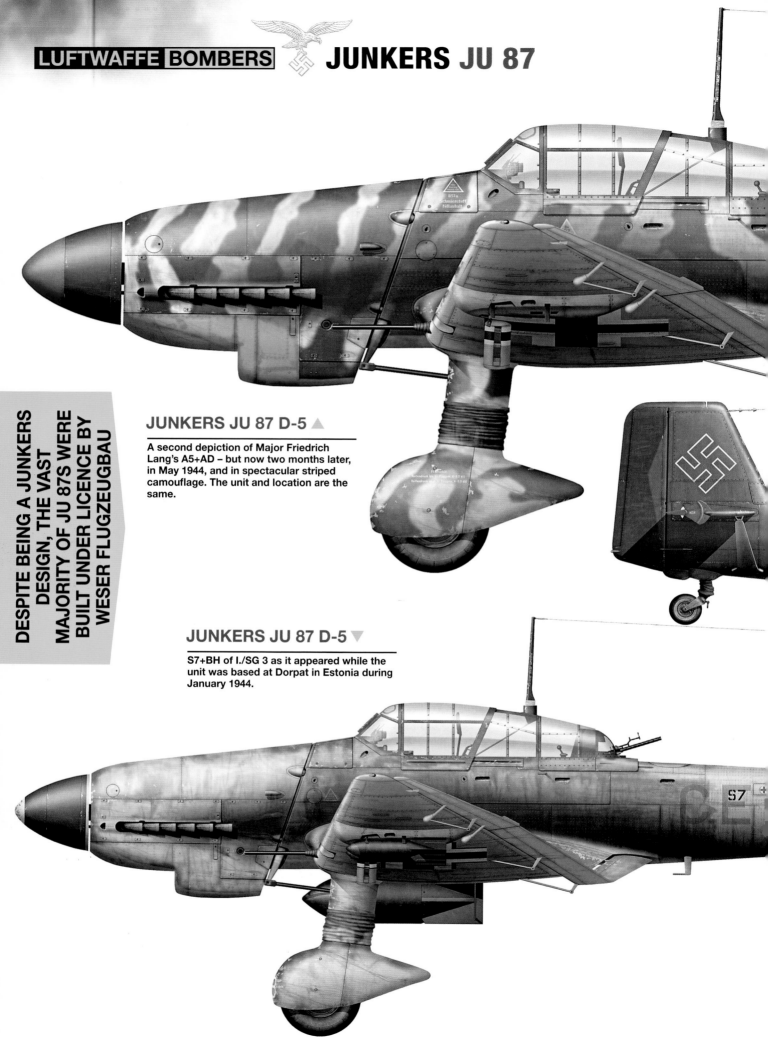

DESPITE BEING A JUNKERS DESIGN, THE VAST MAJORITY OF JU 87S WERE BUILT UNDER LICENCE BY WESER FLUGZEUGBAU

JUNKERS JU 87 D-5 ▲

A second depiction of Major Friedrich Lang's A5+AD – but now two months later, in May 1944, and in spectacular striped camouflage. The unit and location are the same.

JUNKERS JU 87 D-5 ▼

S7+BH of I./SG 3 as it appeared while the unit was based at Dorpat in Estonia during January 1944.

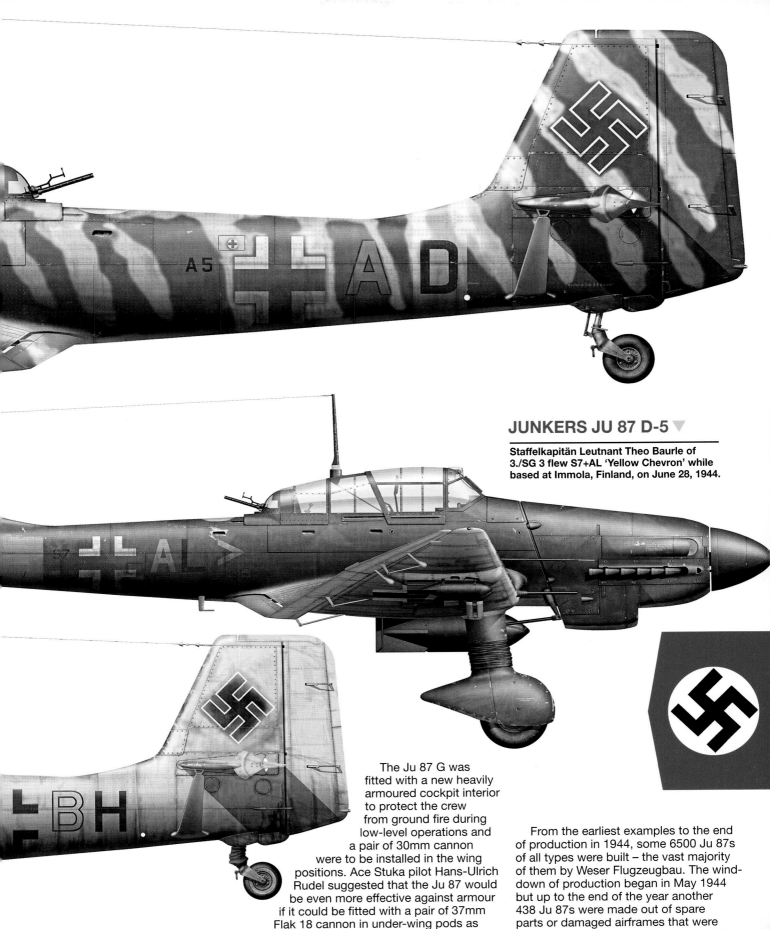

JUNKERS JU 87 D-5 ▼

Staffelkapitän Leutnant Theo Baurle of 3./SG 3 flew S7+AL 'Yellow Chevron' while based at Immola, Finland, on June 28, 1944.

The Ju 87 G was fitted with a new heavily armoured cockpit interior to protect the crew from ground fire during low-level operations and a pair of 30mm cannon were to be installed in the wing positions. Ace Stuka pilot Hans-Ulrich Rudel suggested that the Ju 87 would be even more effective against armour if it could be fitted with a pair of 37mm Flak 18 cannon in under-wing pods as the Bordkanone BK 3,7. These were duly fitted to a D-1 during January 1943 and the arrangement was formalised as the Ju 87 G-1 in April 1943. Most G-1s were created by rebuilding old D-1 and D-2 series airframes while converted D-5 airframes were given the designation G-2. A total of 208 Ju 87 Gs were put together.

From the earliest examples to the end of production in 1944, some 6500 Ju 87s of all types were built – the vast majority of them by Weser Flugzeugbau. The wind-down of production began in May 1944 but up to the end of the year another 438 Ju 87s were made out of spare parts or damaged airframes that were reconditioned using new parts.

While it might have owed its inception to the disintegration of Heinkel's speedy but delicate He 118 at the hands of Ernst Udet, the Ju 87 was able to demonstrate time and again when it came to close-support and ground-attack missions it was the right aircraft for the job. ●

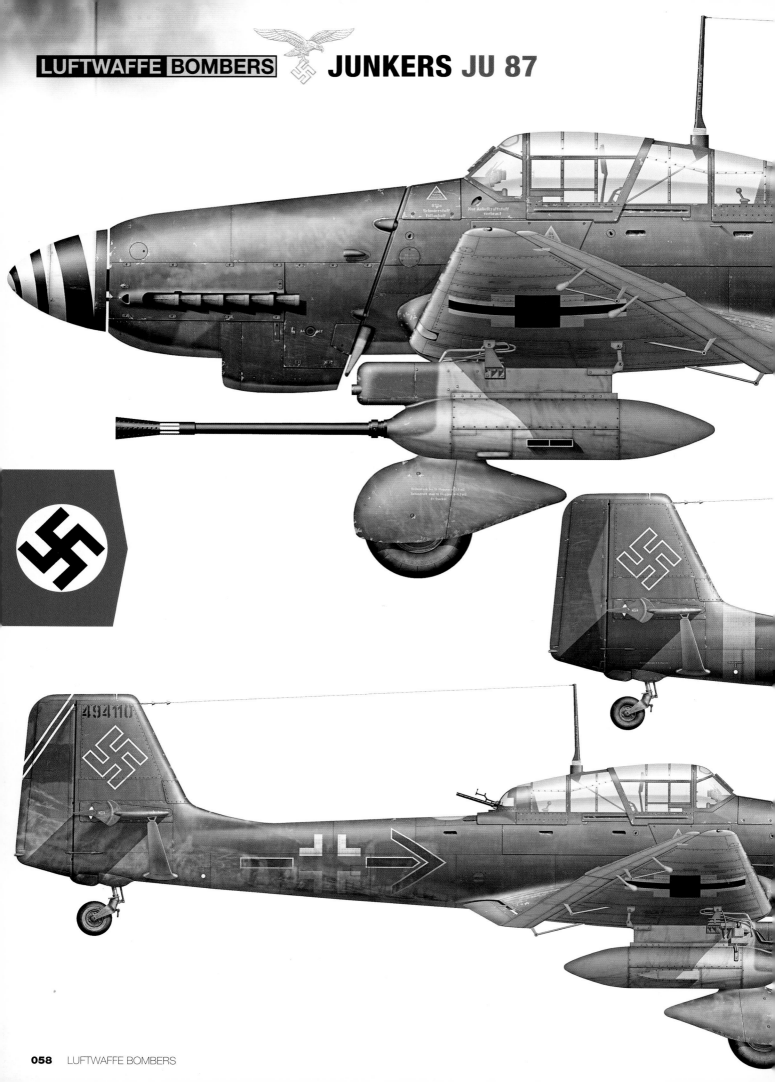

494110

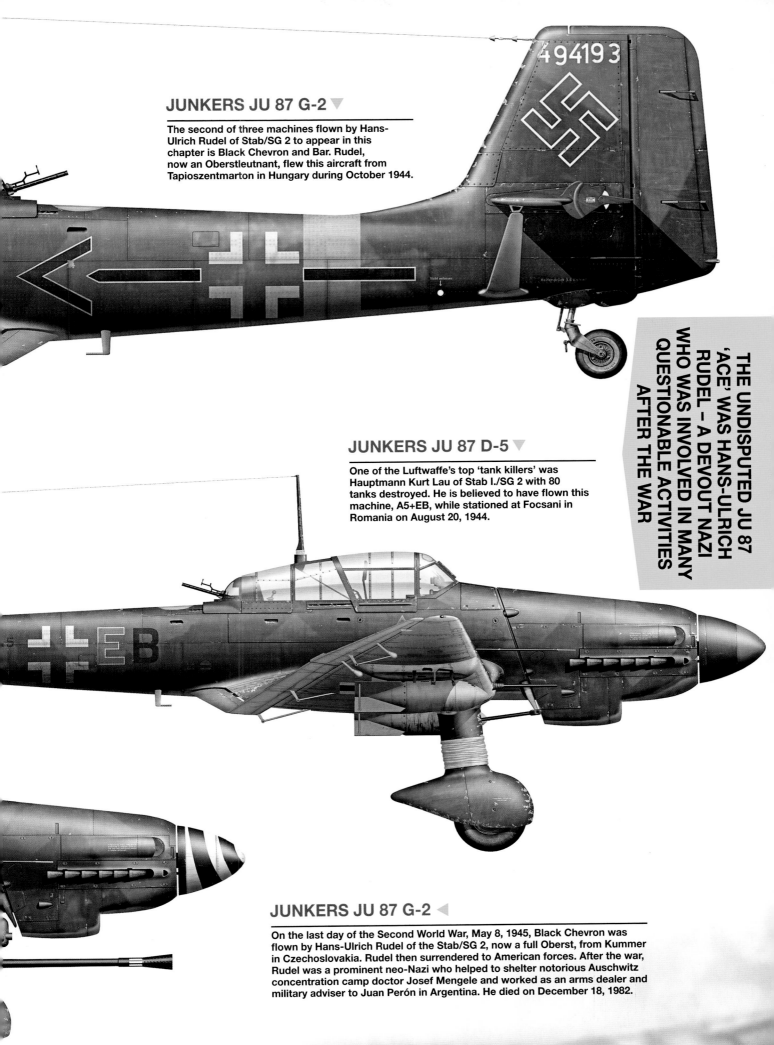

JUNKERS JU 87 G-2 ▼

The second of three machines flown by Hans-Ulrich Rudel of Stab/SG 2 to appear in this chapter is Black Chevron and Bar. Rudel, now an Oberstleutnant, flew this aircraft from Tapioszentmarton in Hungary during October 1944.

JUNKERS JU 87 D-5 ▼

One of the Luftwaffe's top 'tank killers' was Hauptmann Kurt Lau of Stab I./SG 2 with 80 tanks destroyed. He is believed to have flown this machine, A5+EB, while stationed at Focsani in Romania on August 20, 1944.

THE UNDISPUTED JU 87 'ACE' WAS HANS-ULRICH RUDEL – A DEVOUT NAZI WHO WAS INVOLVED IN MANY QUESTIONABLE ACTIVITIES AFTER THE WAR

JUNKERS JU 87 G-2 ◀

On the last day of the Second World War, May 8, 1945, Black Chevron was flown by Hans-Ulrich Rudel of the Stab/SG 2, now a full Oberst, from Kummer in Czechoslovakia. Rudel then surrendered to American forces. After the war, Rudel was a prominent neo-Nazi who helped to shelter notorious Auschwitz concentration camp doctor Josef Mengele and worked as an arms dealer and military adviser to Juan Perón in Argentina. He died on December 18, 1982.

MESSERSCHMITT ME 109

The legendary Messerschmitt Bf 109 needs no introduction as a fighter but it also saw use as a fighter-bomber. Its diminutive size, narrow undercarriage and low payload capacity did not naturally lend themselves to bombing operations but nevertheless a number of bomb-carrying variants were produced and saw action.

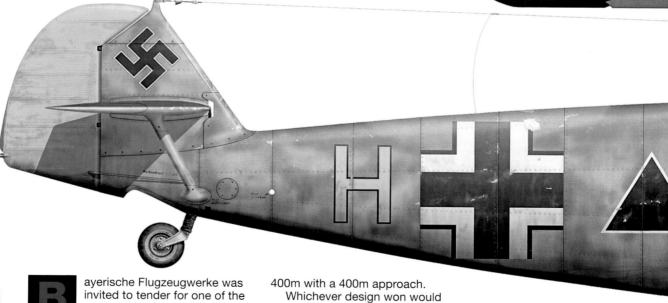

1935-1945

Bayerische Flugzeugwerke was invited to tender for one of the earliest RLM requirements in July 1933 – for a new single-seat fighter with two forward-firing machine guns that could do 400km/h for 20 minutes at 6000m and stay in the air for an hour.

It also had to be suitable for pilots of average ability, easy to recover from a spin, capable of flying in fog and cloud, small enough to transport by rail, have protection against leakage of fuel and be able to land on an airfield of 400m by 400m with a 400m approach.

Whichever design won would essentially become the Luftwaffe's new standard fighter and as such the contract was particularly sought-after.

A mock-up of Bayerische Flugzeugwerke's entry was inspected in January 1935 and the type received the RLM designation Bf 109. The other competitors were the Arado Ar 80, Heinkel's He 112 and later Focke-Wulf's Fw 159.

Eventually the field was narrowed down to just the He 112 and Bf 109. The former

MITT

MESSERSCHMITT BF 109 E-4/B ▲

On the opening day of the invasion of the Soviet Union, June 22, 1941, Yellow F was serving with 6.(Schl.)/LG 2, stationed at Praschnitz in Poland. The unit flew into Soviet airspace during the early hours of the morning and attacked some of the 60 airfields earmarked for the initial assault before providing fighter support for other ground-attack units. A total of 1400 Soviet aircraft were destroyed on the ground during this first day of combat operations.

MESSERSCHMITT BF 109 E-4/B ▼

Yellow H of 6.(Schl.)/LG 2, stationed at Vitbesk, USSR, took part in bombing operations against counter-attacking Soviet forces in the vicinity of Smolensk during late July 1941. In just a few days the unit lost four Bf 109 Es, with one pilot lost and listed as MIA, and a further five suffered damage.

could turn better but the latter was faster and more agile when it came to aerobatic manoeuvres. A head-to-head contest commenced on February 8, 1936, and by March 12 the Bf 109 had edged ahead to become the RLM's preferred design. By September the competition was over and Bayerische Flugzeugwerke received a production contract for its 109.

Just 22 Bf 109 As, powered by the Jumo 210 B, were constructed before production switched to the Jumo 210 D-powered B-series. During the spring of 1938 production switched again to the Jumo 210 G-engined Bf 109 C, and again to the Jumo 210 D-powered Bf 109 D in mid-1938.

So far, not a single Bf 109 had been built as a fighter-bomber. All versions had been pure fighters with a variety of different machine gun and cannon arrangements. This was to change with the next evolution of the Bf 109 – the E-series.

This was the first Bf 109 to be made in

MESSERSCHMITT BF 109 E-4/B ◀

By July 1941, II.(Schl.)/LG 2 had been reduced to just 14 combat ready aircraft – having begun Operation Barbarossa with 38 Bf 109s and 22 Hs 123s. Among the surviving machines was Red M of 5.(Schl.)/LG 2. It is shown here as it appeared at Spaskaya in the USSR during August 1941.

truly astonishing numbers and in a wide variety of sub-types. The Bf 109 E entered production in late 1938. Again, the biggest change was a new engine – the Jumo 210 being replaced by the Daimler-Benz DB 601 A. It was longer and 400lb heavier but it gave the Bf 109 a respectable 1085hp, compared to the Jumo 210's 690hp. The basic E-1 fighter was followed by the E-2 which had an MG FF 20mm autocannon in the engine and two more in the wings. The E-3 deleted the engine cannon but kept the other two.

The latest Bf 109 when the Battle of Britain began was the E-4, with MG FF/M wing cannon and better headrest armour for the pilot. This was the first Bf 109 to be offered with the capability to carry bombs as the fighter-bomber Bf 109 E-4/B and E-4/BN. The former had a DB 601 Aa engine, while the latter had a DB 601 N. Both were able to carry either a single SC 250 or up to four SC 50s on a rack between their wings.

The E-5 and E-6 were reconnaissance versions but the E-7, the first Bf 109 capable of carrying a drop tank, could also be used as a fighter-bomber if the centreline tank was replaced with a bomb.

The next major Bf 109 revision was the F-series – which was the standard fighter of the Luftwaffe as the invasion of the Soviet Union, Operation Barbarossa, commenced on June 22, 1941. The F improved on the E in almost every respect, with wing-mounted weaponry being deleted entirely in favour of a single engine-mounted MG FF/M 20mm cannon and the two cowling MG 17s. The engine cowling was redesigned to become more aerodynamically efficient and the propeller spinner was enlarged to blend smoothly into the cowling.

Armour protection for the pilot's head was improved again and his seat was reshaped and became non-adjustable. A new self-sealing fuel tank was also provided, the hydraulic system was redesigned, the radiator flaps became thermostatically controlled and the oil cooler was enlarged.

Other alterations included a reduction

MESSERSCHMITT BF 109 F-4/B ▲

Oberleutnant Frank Liesendahl of 10.(Jabo)/JG 2 flew Blue 1 from Beaumont-le-Roger, France, on March 31, 1942. Just three and a half months later, on July 17, 1942, he was shot down and killed south-east of Brixton, London.

in rudder area, the horizontal tailplanes were repositioned down and forward and lost their bracing struts, the tailwheel became semi-retractable and the undercarriage mainwheel legs were angled forward by six degrees to improve handling while taxiing. The tail structure was also reinforced and the wings were also redesigned.

It was intended that the Bf 109 F should be powered by the new DB 601 E but this was initially unavailable so pre-production F-0 machines, F-1s and F-2s received the DB 601 N.

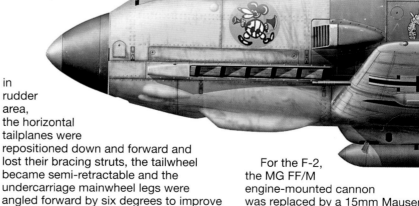

For the F-2, the MG FF/M engine-mounted cannon was replaced by a 15mm Mauser MG 151 cannon – which itself was replaced by the 20mm version of the same gun as it began to become available. The F-3 finally saw the introduction of the DB 601 E – though only 15 were made. The F-4 also had the DB 601 E but had the same armament as the F-2, including its new MG 151 20mm cannon.

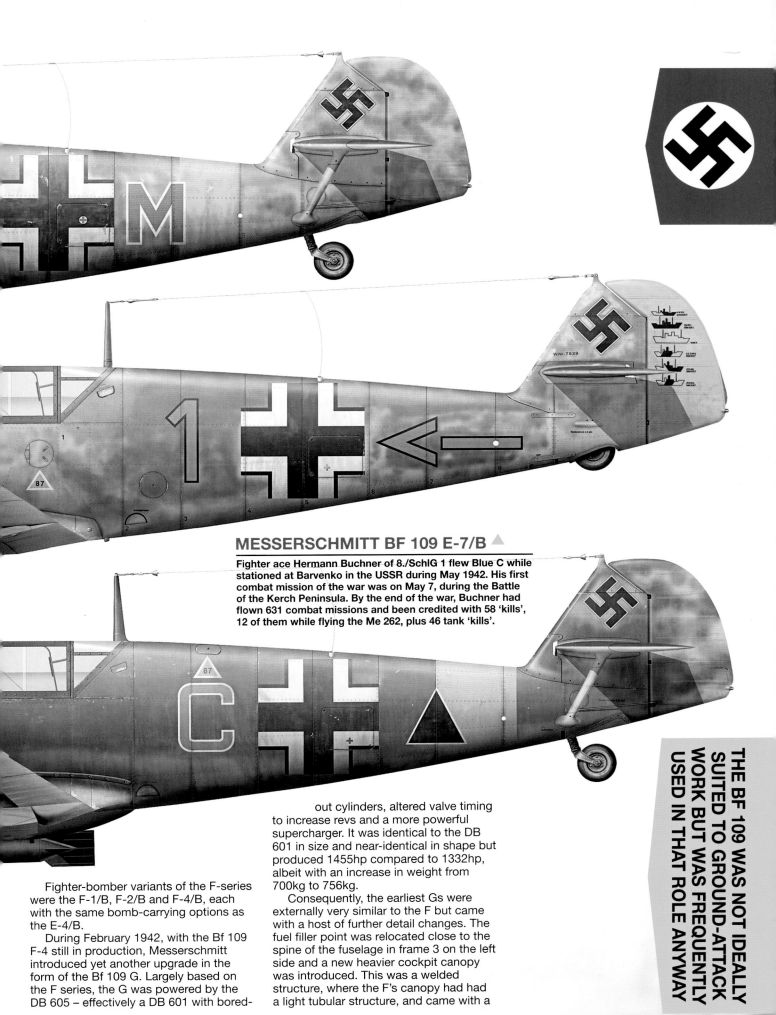

MESSERSCHMITT BF 109 E-7/B ▲

Fighter ace Hermann Buchner of 8./SchIG 1 flew Blue C while stationed at Barvenko in the USSR during May 1942. His first combat mission of the war was on May 7, during the Battle of the Kerch Peninsula. By the end of the war, Buchner had flown 631 combat missions and been credited with 58 'kills', 12 of them while flying the Me 262, plus 46 tank 'kills'.

Fighter-bomber variants of the F-series were the F-1/B, F-2/B and F-4/B, each with the same bomb-carrying options as the E-4/B.

During February 1942, with the Bf 109 F-4 still in production, Messerschmitt introduced yet another upgrade in the form of the Bf 109 G. Largely based on the F series, the G was powered by the DB 605 – effectively a DB 601 with bored-

out cylinders, altered valve timing to increase revs and a more powerful supercharger. It was identical to the DB 601 in size and near-identical in shape but produced 1455hp compared to 1332hp, albeit with an increase in weight from 700kg to 756kg.

Consequently, the earliest Gs were externally very similar to the F but came with a host of further detail changes. The fuel filler point was relocated close to the spine of the fuselage in frame 3 on the left side and a new heavier cockpit canopy was introduced. This was a welded structure, where the F's canopy had had a light tubular structure, and came with a built-in armour glass windscreen.

A windscreen washer was also introduced in the form of a small tube which ran along the screen and could spray fuel onto the glass to clear away oil or other obstructions. Ventilation scoops were introduced below the windscreen too. Unpressurised Bf 109 Gs usually also had a rectangular ventilation inlet on either side of the cockpit, although these were sometimes sealed up or omitted altogether.

A deeper oil radiator was now fitted and emergency shut-off valves were installed which would allow the pilot to isolate the wing radiators in the event of a coolant leak – to prevent the vital fluid completely draining away, which would result in near-instantaneous engine seizure. The tailwheel of the G could also be locked in position to make take-offs and landings easier.

Practical operational experience was also applied to the Bf 109's cockpit instrumentation, with a combined artificial horizon/turn and slip indicator replacing what had previously been just a turn and slip indicator.

The Bf 109 G was offered in a huge array of different versions with many further modifications and it falls beyond the scope of this publication to list them all. However, any of them could become a fighter-bomber with either an R-1 or R-2 Rüstsatz or field modification pack. The former involved the fitment of an ETC 900/IXb rack for carrying SC 250 bombs, while the latter included an ETC 50/VIId rack for four SC 50 bombs.

Production of the final Bf 109 of the war, the K-series, commenced in late 1944, with the only version to see quantity production being the K-4. This could be distinguished from earlier models by a relocation of the radio equipment hatch to a position higher up between frames four and five, and a repositioning of the fuselage fuel tank filler point to between frames two and three. The D/F loop moved rearwards to a point between frames three and four on the fuselage spine. The Bf 109 K-4 rudder had a Flettner tab as standard and a long, fully retractable tailwheel was added; the wheel itself measuring 350 x 135mm. Two small doors closed over the tailwheel recess to provide a smooth aerodynamic form.

There were large rectangular fairings for the type's big 660 x 190mm main undercarriage wheels and doors covered the wheels when they were retracted – though these were often removed by front line units. The K-4 was fitted with a FuG 16ZY radio set, the aerial extending from the underside of the port outer wing, a FuG 25a IFF and FuG 125 Hermine D/F equipment.

Standard armament was an engine-mounted MK 108 or MG 151/20 and a pair of MG 131s in the nose with 300 rounds per gun. As with the G-series, the K could carry four SC 50s or a single SC 250 when kitted out with the appropriate field modification set.

While there is no doubt that Bf 109 pilots flying 'jabo' versions were able to drop their bombs accurately, the aircraft itself was not usually armoured against ground fire and its legendary manoeuvrability suffered greatly when encumbered with the extra load. On the Eastern Front and Mediterranean Theatre, as with every other Luftwaffe ground-attack aircraft, the Bf 109 jabo could be effective – but in the West it seldom had the opportunity to make an impact due to the threat posed by high-performance enemy fighters. ●

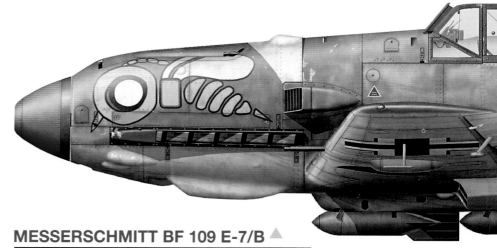

MESSERSCHMITT BF 109 E-7/B ▲

This colourful Bf 109, S9+AS, flew with 8./ZG 1 while the unit was based at Belgorod, USSR, in June 1942.

MESSERSCHMITT BF 109 G-14/AS ▼

Former He 111 pilot Othmar Schwendmayer flew Red 8 of 2./EJG 2, based at Schleswig-Jagel, Germany, against rapidly advancing British, American and Russian forces during the final three weeks of the war. His final mission was on May 4, 1945, when he attacked columns of enemy vehicles on the Hamburg-Lübeck autobahn. Most of his missions were flown at night and he later reported that he believed they had been ineffective.

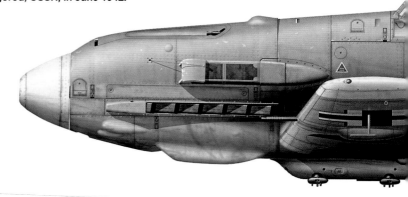

MESSERSCHMITT BF 109 E-7/B TROP ▲

S9+IR of 7./ZG 1, as it appeared in desert camouflage while stationed at Bir el Abd, Egypt, during August 1942.

MESSERSCHMITT BF 109 E-4/B ◄

Major Alfred Druschel of Stab I./SG 1 flew Double Black Chevron during September 1942. Although his units operated primarily in the ground-attack role, Druschel nevertheless managed to achieve seven aerial victories. While taking part in Operation Bodenplatte on January 1, 1945, Druschel led an attack on St Trond airfield in Belgium. He became separated from his formation following a heavy flak attack however, and remains missing to this day.

EASY-FIT MODIFICATION PACKS MEANT ALMOST ANY BF 109 COULD BECOME A FIGHTER-BOMBER IF NECESSARY

JUNKERS

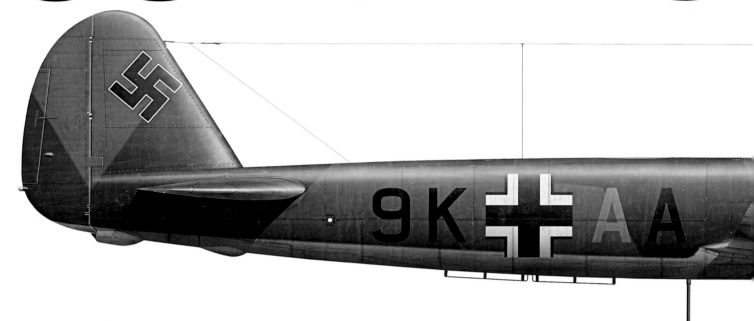

JUNKERS JU 88 A-1 ▶

4D+CH was serving with 1./KG 30, based at Aalborg-West, Denmark, on August 15, 1940, when some 50 Ju 88s were sent to bomb airfields in the north of England. The raid achieved little other than damaging two airfields for the loss of eight He 111s, eight Bf 110s and seven Ju 88s. 4D+CH was not among them, however, surviving until September 1942 when it was shot down.

1936-1945

The Ju 88 was intended as a fast bomber from the start but its intermediate size, flexible design and ease of manufacture made it one of the most adaptable and widely used bomber aircraft of the war.

W hen Germany's air force was being rearmed during the early to mid-1930s, it was decided that in addition to a fast single-seat fighter, a medium bomber, a heavy bomber and a specialised dive-bomber, there should also be a Kampfzerstörer – a twin-engine two-seater multirole aircraft able to operate as either heavy fighter or bomber as the situation required.

Arado, Gotha, Focke-Wulf, Henschel and Messerschmitt were invited to submit tenders for the new aircraft type in 1934 and following the receipt of tenders the latter three were given development contracts.

Focke-Wulf's design was the Fw 57, Henschel built the Hs 124 which was similar to the Fw 57 in layout, and Messerschmitt constructed the Bf 110. The size difference between the three projects was dramatic – the Fw 57 was 16.4m long with a 25m wingspan, the Hs 124 was 14.5m long with an 18.2m

JU 88

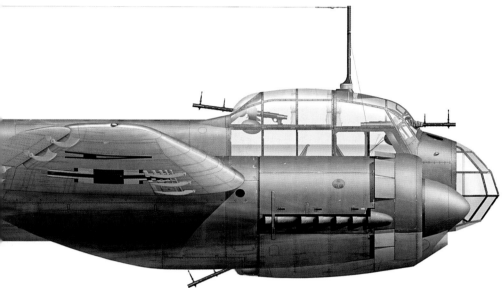

wingspan and the Bf 110 was just 12.3m long with a span of 16.3m.

When these three very different aircraft were assessed, it became clear that the Kampfzerstörer concept was just too broad. None of the tendered designs was suitable for the range of roles it would be expected to fulfil. But rather than altering the designs, it was decided that the requirement itself was at fault – the Kampfzerstörer was split in two, with new separate requirements being drawn up in

mid-1935 for a Zerstörer or 'heavy fighter' and a Schnellbomber or 'fast bomber'.

The Focke-Wulf and Henschel designs were deemed incapable of meeting either requirement and were dismissed, leaving only the Bf 110 in the running for the Zerstörer contract, which it won unopposed. A slightly enlarged version of the Bf 110, the Bf 162, was designed to compete as a Schnellbomber against two new designs – the Junkers Ju 88, initially known as the EF 59, and the Henschel Hs 127.

Junkers was different from the other companies in being publicly owned. Where Messerschmitt and Henschel,

both private companies, were driven by a desire for profit, Junkers was like Arado in being a wholly-owned tool of the German government. If a development competition was won by Junkers, the German government was effectively deciding to develop the aircraft in-house.

The EF 59 was a straightforward design which rejected risky features in favour of practicality; a mock-up was inspected in June 1936 and approved, with Junkers being ordered to produce a series of five prototypes.

Messerschmitt had already received an order for Bf 162 prototypes, but Junkers was able to turn the Ju 88 V1 around faster and get it into the air ahead

JUNKERS JU 88

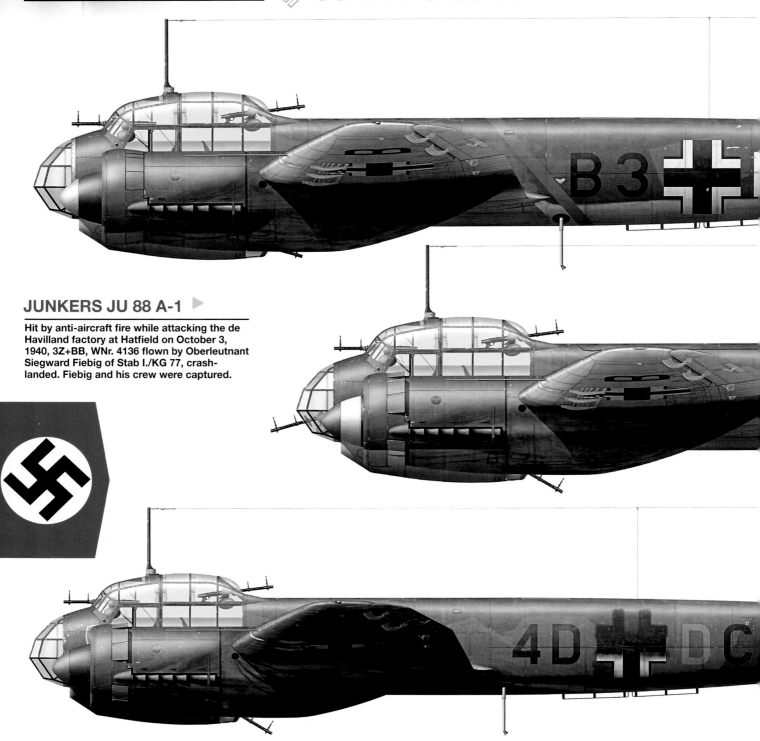

JUNKERS JU 88 A-1 ▶

Hit by anti-aircraft fire while attacking the de Havilland factory at Hatfield on October 3, 1940, 3Z+BB, WNr. 4136 flown by Oberleutnant Siegward Fiebig of Stab I./KG 77, crash-landed. Fiebig and his crew were captured.

of the Bf 162 V1 – on December 12, 1936, powered by a pair of DB 600 A engines. Even as this work was ongoing, however, the RLM decided that the original Schnellbomber specification was inadequate and made several major revisions. The number of crew increased from three to four, the defensive position requirement was altered, fuel capacity was altered, de-icing provision for the wings became essential and most significant of all, the aircraft now had to be capable of dive-bombing.

These revisions were passed on to

Junkers and Messerschmitt in August 1937 – after the Ju 88 V1 and Bf 162 V1 had already undergone flight-testing. In fact, the Ju 88 V1 was badly damaged in a crash on April 10, 1937, the V2 made its first flight later that month and construction of the V3, which incorporated a host of alterations, was already well under way. Therefore, it was expected that the necessary alterations would be incorporated into the V4 and V5. Henschel had been eliminated from the competition by this point.

The Ju 88 V3 first flew on September

13, 1937, fitted with 1000hp Jumo 211 A engines. It also had an enlarged rudder and a Lofte bomb sight, and the rear section of the cockpit was modified to allow for the fitment of a rear-firing gun position.

In January 1938, the Ju 88 was chosen to become the Luftwaffe's new Schnellbomber. Being closely based on the Bf 110, the Bf 162 had struggled to meet the revised requirement – particularly when it came to dive-bombing. The V4 made its first flight on February 2, 1938. This had wing

JUNKERS JU 88 A-1 ◀

During a mission on August 21, 1940, B3+BM, WNr. 6086 flown by Oberfeldwebel Heinz Apollony of 4./KG 54, based at Coulommiers, France, was intercepted by Hurricanes of 17 Squadron and damaged to the extent that it was forced to make a belly landing at 4.15pm on Marsh Farm, Earnley, West Sussex.

JUNKERS JU 88 A-1 ◀

The largest bombing raid mounted against London during the war took place on the night of April 16/17, 1941. Among the 685 aircraft taking part was 4D+DC of Stab II./KG 30, based at Gilze-Rijen, Holland. A total of 66 boroughs were hit with high-explosives, incendiaries and a large number of parachute mines. Some 2000 separate fires were started and St Paul's Cathedral was damaged, along with the Houses of Parliament and the National Gallery. Hundreds of private homes were also damaged or destroyed and some 1000 people were killed – most of them civilians.

de-icing and an elongated fuselage forward section which put the entire cockpit ahead of the leading edge of the wings. It was also the first Ju 88 to feature the type's characteristic glazed nose, plus a gondola was added to the right of the forward fuselage which would house the fourth crewman. This was another defensive position, with the gunner lying flat in the gondola to operate a machine gun firing down and to the rear.

On February 24, an attempt was made to set a new speed record with the Ju 88 V3 – the additional power of the Jumo 211s meant that it could easily outpace the two earlier DB 600-powered airframes – but the attempt ended in disaster when the aircraft was destroyed in a crash which killed everyone on board.

The V5 made its maiden flight on April 13, powered by Jumo 211 Bs, which made 1200hp each. It was intended as the guinea pig for dive-bombing trials and as such had a solid nose, a low-profile cockpit and no gondola.

The Ju 88's fuselage was lengthened again for the sixth prototype – the V6 being intended to provide the basis for the first production model. It also featured redesigned landing gear, four-bladed propellers, two internal bomb bays and slightly larger horizontal tail surfaces. This first flew on June 18, 1938. V7 was a test-bed for fixed forward-firing guns and V8 tested Kutonase barrage balloon cutting gear.

Work on a series of seven pre-production aircraft was begun in January 1939, although these were destined to be designated Ju 88 V9 to V15, rather than A-0s. These were built in parallel with another 14 aircraft, making a total of 21 pre-production machines. The first A-1 series then followed in August. By the end of 1939, a total of 109 Ju 88s had been built – with contributions

from both Henschel and Arado as sub-contracted production began. Three further subcontractors came on-stream in January 1940: Dornier, ATG and Siebel. And they were joined by Heinkel the following month.

The Ju 88 A-2 was the same as the A-1 but with Jumo 211 G-1 engines fitted and the option to fit jettisonable rocket packs to help with takeoff when the aircraft was overloaded. The A-3 was a conversion trainer with dual controls and the A-4 represented a complete upgrade from the A-1, with new engines – the Jumo 211 J – a longer wingspan and a strengthened aircraft which enabled the aircraft to carry heavy loads.

The A-4 also had modified rear gun mountings to improve the rearward field of fire plus an aiming window made from bulletproof glass to protect the gunner. The canopy itself was bulged outwards to the rear, creating a 'double bubble' effect. All of the aircraft's guns were now specified as belt-fed MG 81s rather than magazine-fed MG 15s to remove the hassle of reloading.

JUNKERS JU 88

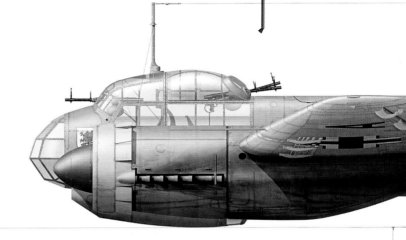

JUNKERS JU 88 A-10 ▶

Flown by Major Friedrich-Karl Knust of the
Stab./LG 1, based at Krumovo, Bulgaria,
L1+AA was photographed by correspondents
for bi-weekly propaganda magazine *Der Adler*
on a return flight from Africa on September
25, 1941. This is how it looked at the time.

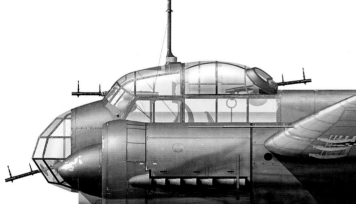

JUNKERS JU 88 A-4 ▶

Hauptmann Heinrich Hahn of Stab
I./KG 51 flew 9K+FB, WNr. 1050 while
stationed at Bagerovo in the USSR on
November 3, 1941. Hahn was killed
when his Ju 88 crashed at Tirasol
airfield on February 3, 1942.

JUNKERS JU 88 A-5 ◄

This A-5, L1+GN of 5./LG 1, was stationed at Athens-Eleusis, Greece, during May 1941. Engine cowlings were painted yellow as per official instructions.

JUNKERS JU 88 A-5 ◄

I. and III./KG 77 flew missions in support of Operation Barbarossa with an initial total of 59 Ju 88s. By October 1941, the units were involved in the Battle of Leningrad, with 3Z+AB, WNr. 3558 being flown by Hauptmann Joachim Pötter of Stab I./KG 77, from Siwerskaya in the USSR. This is how the aircraft appeared on October 25, 1941, when Pötter was shot down by a Soviet fighter. He made a forced landing near Raguj and despite being injured managed to make it back to German lines.

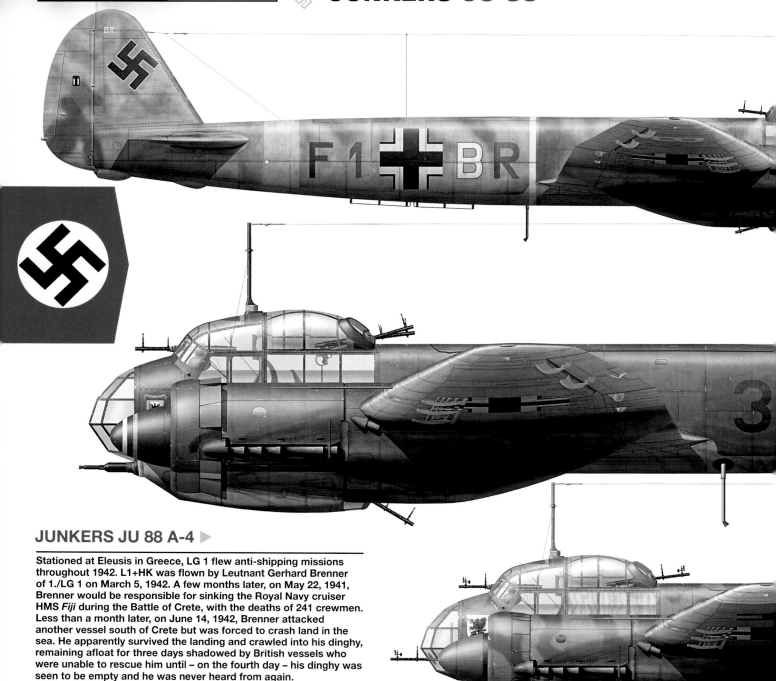

JUNKERS JU 88 A-4 ▶

Stationed at Eleusis in Greece, LG 1 flew anti-shipping missions throughout 1942. L1+HK was flown by Leutnant Gerhard Brenner of 1./LG 1 on March 5, 1942. A few months later, on May 22, 1941, Brenner would be responsible for sinking the Royal Navy cruiser HMS *Fiji* during the Battle of Crete, with the deaths of 241 crewmen. Less than a month later, on June 14, 1942, Brenner attacked another vessel south of Crete but was forced to crash land in the sea. He apparently survived the landing and crawled into his dinghy, remaining afloat for three days shadowed by British vessels who were unable to rescue him until – on the fourth day – his dinghy was seen to be empty and he was never heard from again.

However, teething troubles with the Jumo 211 J meant that the A-5 was actually introduced slightly earlier than the A-4, in late 1940. This featured some of the A-4's upgrades, such as the greater wingspan, but retained the earlier Jumo 211 B-1, G-1 or H-1 engines for the sake of reliability. The A-6 was an A-5 fitted with balloon cutting gear and the A-7 was the dual control trainer version of the A-5.

The earliest reconnaissance versions of the Ju 88 were the A-1 (F) and A-5 (F), which were largely the same as the A-1 and A-5 except for the installation of camera equipment. A dedicated reconnaissance machine, the D-2, appeared in early 1941. This had the Ju 88's usual dive brakes removed and camera gear installed

– but it was still based on the A-5 as the Jumo 211 J was still experiencing development problems.

Also during 1940, development efforts were concentrated on the Ju 88 B – regarded as the next overall upgrade. This would end up being put on the back burner before going on to a second life later as the Ju 188 (see p118-121).

At the start of 1941, Ju 88 production had reached more than 200 aircraft a month, mostly A-5 and D-2s. The A-4 bomber, and its D-1 reconnaissance version, finally entered production in February 1941 – a year later than expected. The A-1/A-5/A-4 pattern of designations was continued when tropicalised versions with engine filters were planned, with A-9, A-10

and A-11 corresponding to each, just as the A-3, A-7 and A-12 trainer versions also corresponded.

Up to this point, it had been hoped that the Ju 88 would be replaced by the winner of the Bomber B competition. Junkers' own entry, the Ju 288, had been a favourite to win. There had seemed little point in continuing to develop the basic Ju 88 beyond the A-4 when it was likely to be succeeded by the Ju 288, with even the Ju 88 B having been shelved for this reason. However, by early 1942 it was clear that the engines upon which the 288 relied were not coming, so plans for the Ju 188 were drawn up and production of the Ju 88 A-4 and D-1 – and the fighter

JUNKERS JU 88 A-5 ◄

Before the Second World War, Dieter Lukesch had been a pilot with the Austrian Luftwaffe and then joined the German Luftwaffe. He flew F1+BR with 7./KG 76 during November-December 1941 from Orscha in the USSR. Later on, on Christmas Day, 1944, he led a group of eight jet-propelled Arado Ar 234s on a bombing mission over Liege in Belgium – the first combat operation by dedicated jet-propelled aircraft in history. After the war, he worked as an airline pilot for Lufthansa.

JUNKERS JU 88 A-4 ▼

3Z+ER, WNr. 3604 of 7./KG 77, was wrecked during a crash-landing near Dubrovnik on February 8, 1942.

SO MANY A-4S WERE BUILT THAT MANY WERE LATER RECYCLED INTO DIFFERENT ROLES

version based on the same platform, the C-6, was prolonged indefinitely. Three companies dropped out of Ju 88 production – Arado, Dornier and Heinkel – while the remainder, Junkers itself, Henschel, ATG and Siebel, ramped up their output.

During 1943, a number of factory modification kits were developed which could be used to equip a standard A-4 for particular roles. The A-4 LT was a torpedo carrier, the S-1 was an A-4 better suited to the type's original Schnellbomber role and the T-1 was a reconnaissance machine. The R-1 and R-2 were both fighters, with the R-2 being basically a Ju 88 C-6 but with BMW 801 engines.

The latter were constructed without night fighter equipment, as heavy fighters, and this had to be added afterwards. Deliveries of the first dedicated night fighter version, the Ju 88 G-1, commenced in December 1943. Once production of the Ju 188 E-1 bomber and the reconnaissance model Ju 188 F-1 commenced Junkers itself ceased production of the A-4 and D-1, though these models continued to be produced by the other three companies.

Also during 1943, many older A-4s were converted to new, more specialised, roles using modification packs – for example, Ju 88 A-17 torpedo bombers were created using A-4s with a number of wing alterations and retrofitted with torpedo control systems, and torpedo

racks. A new ground-attack variant, the P-series, was created by adding heavy cannon to existing A-4s.

The P-1 was fitted with an under-fuselage 75mm cannon, the P-2 and P-3 with 37mm cannon and the P-4 with a 50mm cannon. The largest weapon ever mounted on a Ju 88 was the recoilless 88mm Düsenkanone, but although this was tested it never reached production.

The dramatic conversion of a D-1 to Ju 88 H-1 status involved the insertion of two new fuselage sections – one ahead of the wing and one behind it. The H-1 was a long-range reconnaissance version and needed the fuselage extensions to accommodate large internal fuel tanks. In addition, it was powered by BMW 801s, these replacing the D-1's Jumos, the under-fuselage weapons gondola was removed and a fixed rearward firing gun

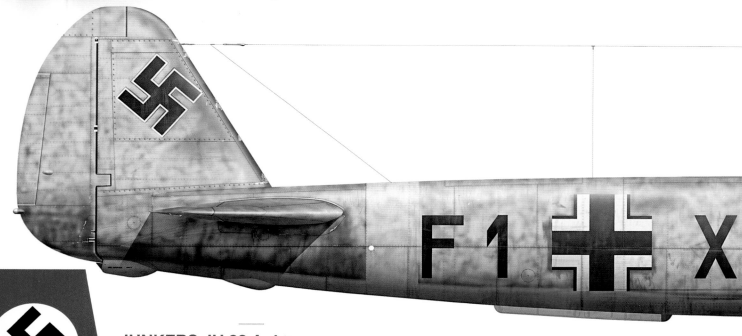

JUNKERS JU 88 A-4 ▶

Hauptmann Sigmund-Ulrich Freiherr von Gravenreuth of Stab II./KG 30 flew 4D+AC WNr. 140171 from Petsamo in Finland during April 1942. Von Gravenreuth retrained to fly single-engine fighters during the autumn of 1944 and died on October 16, 1944, when his Bf 109 crashed.

took its place.

The H-2 was to be a heavy fighter intended as a long-range bomber escort. It featured the same fuselage extensions as the H-1 but had four MG 151s in an under-fuselage weapons pod rather than a set of cameras. It is believed that only one example of this sub-type was completed.

The A-4 was also utilised in the creation of Mistel composite aircraft when paired with either a Me 109 or a Fw 190. The entire cockpit section of the Ju 88 was replaced with a huge shaped explosive charge and long proboscis-like detonator, while the engine and flight controls were routed instead to the fighter which was attached to its back. The fighter's pilot operated the whole contraption and got it airborne. The composite was then flown to its target and, once aimed, the Ju 88 portion was released – with the fighter flying clear. The A-4 was then kept flying straight by an on-board autopilot until it impacted the target.

Those factories still building the A-4 and D-1 were winding down production

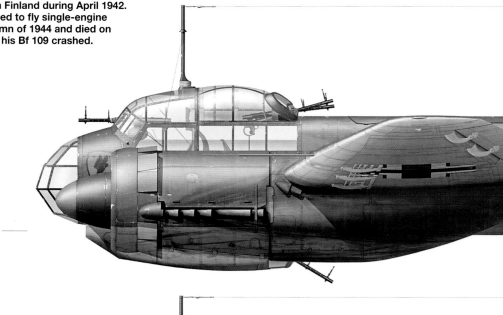

JUNKERS JU 88 A-4 ▶

9K+FK with its additional weapons loadout was flown by Leutnant Dr Karl-Heinz Stahl of 2./KG 51 from Stalino in the USSR during July 1942. Stahl was apparently considered to be a specialist in carrying out specialist one-off attacks on particular targets. Nearly two years earlier, on August 23, 1940, he and his crew had flown a solo raid on the RAE test centre at Farnborough and survived.

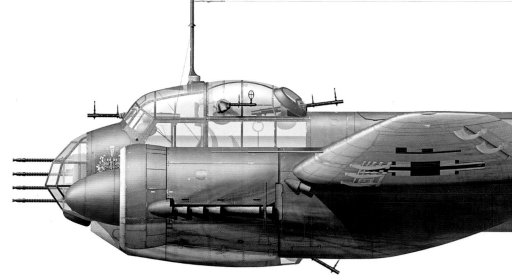

JUNKERS JU 88 C-6 ▶

Something of an imposter in this company, F1+XM was a C-6 fighter variant, but is included due to its unusual paint scheme. The C-6 had a solid nose but F1+XM's was carefully painted with 'frames' and mock transparencies to resemble a glass-nosed bomber – evidently as a means of confusing enemy pilots. The aircraft was flown by 4./KG 76, based at Orscha-Süd, USSR, during March 1942.

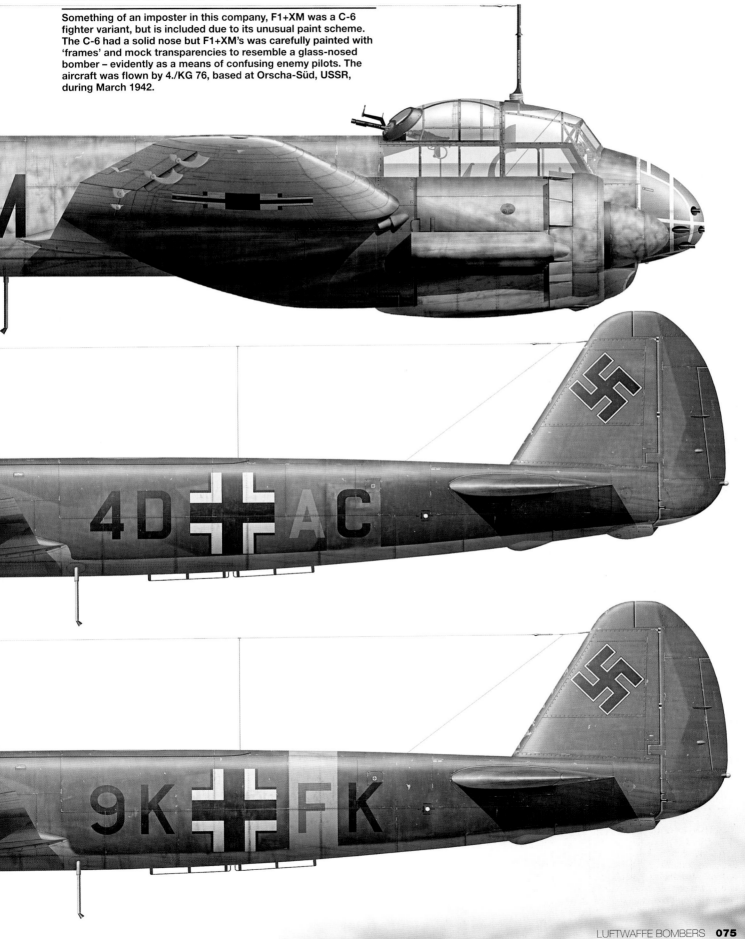

JUNKERS JU 88

JUNKERS JU 88 A-5 ▶

L1+DU was flown by 10./LG 1 while based at Iraklion on Crete during March 1943.

JUNKERS JU 88 A-4 ▶

Hauptmann Klaus Häberlen of Stab I./KG 51 flew 9K+BB from Bagerovo in the USSR during his 300th mission, on April 17, 1943. The aircraft bears the coat of arms of the city of Memmingen. Häberlen was demoted by Göring in October 1943 but returned to staff duties in October 1944. He survived the war and died on April 7, 2002.

SOME 15,000 EXAMPLES OF THE JU 88 WERE BUILT IN TOTAL

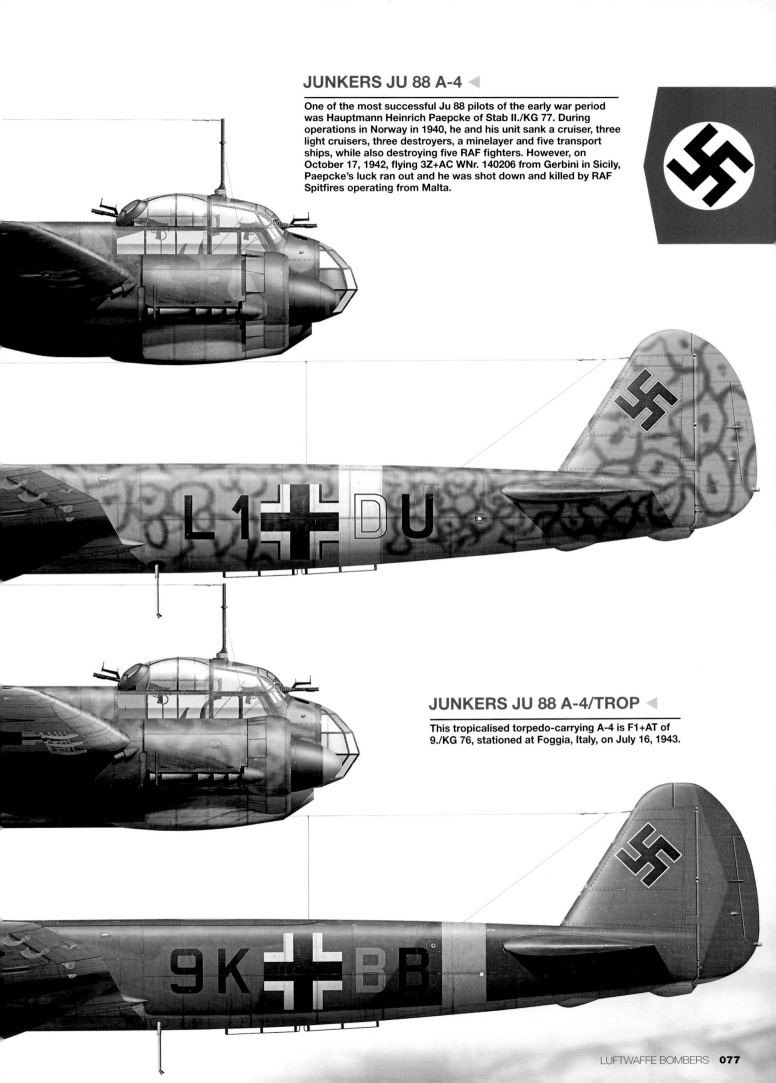

JUNKERS JU 88 A-4 ◄

One of the most successful Ju 88 pilots of the early war period was Hauptmann Heinrich Paepcke of Stab II./KG 77. During operations in Norway in 1940, he and his unit sank a cruiser, three light cruisers, three destroyers, a minelayer and five transport ships, while also destroying five RAF fighters. However, on October 17, 1942, flying 3Z+AC WNr. 140206 from Gerbini in Sicily, Paepcke's luck ran out and he was shot down and killed by RAF Spitfires operating from Malta.

JUNKERS JU 88 A-4/TROP ◄

This tropicalised torpedo-carrying A-4 is F1+AT of 9./KG 76, stationed at Foggia, Italy, on July 16, 1943.

JUNKERS JU 88 S-3 ▼

A lightly armed Schnellbomber, Z6+BH was operated by 1./KG 66 from Celles in Belgium on January 24, 1945.

December 1943, with production being switched to the Ju 188 and Ju 88 G night fighter series. The last A-4s were completed by Henschel and ATG in May 1944, with Henschel then turning its facilities over to the production of the Ju 88 S-3 Schnellbomber, which was powered by Jumo 213s, and ATG switching to production of Ju 388s. Junkers itself continued to turn out Ju 88 G-1s, C-6s and R-2s. Siebel was now building Ju 188s and all Ju 88 models that were powered by the Jumo 213.

When the aircraft production reorganisation implemented by the Jägerstab took effect towards the end of the year, all bomber versions of the Ju 88 and 188 were cancelled. However, the Ju 88 continued in production as the G-6 night fighter well into March 1945. There was even a new sub-type – the G-10 – which had the stretched fuselage of the H-series but the weapons and equipment of the G-6.

The Ju 88 was one of the most numerous aircraft of the war, with more than 15,000 examples having been turned out by May 8, 1945. By way of comparison, only around 6500 He 111s were made and 1900 Do 217s. Its chief characteristic, however, was its versatility. The Ju 88 could be adapted to almost any role and became the ubiquitous workhorse of the Luftwaffe during the war. While it may not have been the fastest, most capacious or most heavily armed aircraft on the German air force's books it was certainly the most adaptable. ●

JUNKERS JU 88 A-17 ▼

Torpedo bomber 1H+FL of 3./KG 26 was photographed in this fetching 'squiggle' pattern camouflage at the unit's base in Bardufoss, Norway, on February 10, 1945. The pattern makes the fuselage cross rather difficult to see.

Having run out of fuel following a bombing run on the southern Italian port of Naples, B3+MH, WNr. 550396, flown by 23-year-old Unteroffizier Drago Verhovc of 1./KG 54, landed at Dübendorf in Switzerland at 10pm on October 21, 1943. Verhovc had tried to return to base but found it impossible to land due to a snowstorm. It was the first Ju 88 to be held by the neutral Swiss authorities and after being repainted with Swiss badges was subjected to a regime of test flights. Verhovc and his crew were returned to their unit on March 17, 1944, following an exchange of Allied prisoners. On May 14, 1944, Verhovc and the same crew failed to return from a bombing mission over Bristol and remain listed as 'missing' today.

DESPITE ALL EFFORTS TO REPLACE IT, THE JU 88 REMAINED IN PRODUCTION UNTIL THE END OF THE WAR

FOCKE-WULF

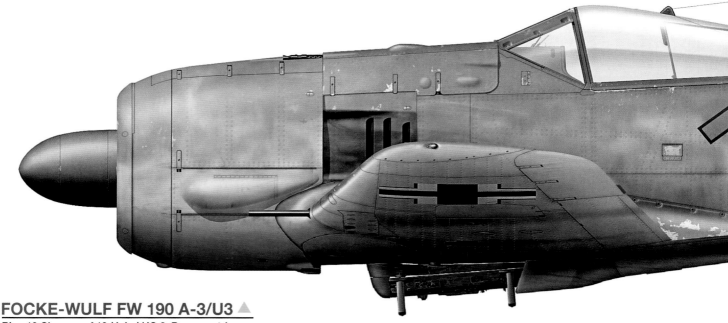

FOCKE-WULF FW 190 A-3/U3 ▲

Blue 13 Chevron of 10.(Jabo)/JG 2, Beaumont-le-Roger, France, May 1942.

FOCKE-WULF FW 190 A-4 ▶

This aircraft, White 1, was flown by Erprobungskommando 19 from Castel Benito in Libya during July 1942 to test the Fw 190 and Bf 109 G/Trop under desert conditions. The unit was disbanded two months later.

1938-1945

The Fw 190 was envisioned as a fighter-bomber from an early stage and with the slow-flying specialised Stukas – the Ju 87 and Hs 123 – becoming increasingly outdated and vulnerable as the war progressed, the Fw 190 was adapted to take on their tactical bombing and ground-attack roles.

The Messerschmitt Bf 109 defeated Focke-Wulf's parasol-wing Fw 159 design in the 1934-35 contest to produce a new standard fighter for the Luftwaffe – but in several key aspects the 109 remained a mid-1930s fighter throughout its service career.

Its undercarriage was narrow, which could make landing tricky, its heavy-framed cockpit canopy reduced visibility and its small wings meant that its ability to carry external stores was severely curtailed.

The RLM soon decided that the Luftwaffe needed a companion for the Bf 109 and Focke-Wulf, having learned from both its own mistakes and the shortcomings of the Messerschmitt design, was able to produce an aircraft with good all-round visibility for the pilot which was durable, fast, easy to land on a

FW 190

wide-track undercarriage and capable of carrying a substantial payload.

The new Fw 190, conceived in 1938, was to be powered by the new air-cooled 1500hp radial 14-cylinder BMW 139. With two rows of seven cylinders mounted back to back, it generated a lot of heat in a small area but offered a high power to weight ratio. It was to drive a three-bladed 3.4m diameter Vereingite Deutsche Metallwerke electro-hydraulic variable pitch propeller. Over this was fitted a large Doppelhaube ducted spinner intended to reduce drag.

Focke-Wulf submitted the design to the RLM and the company was given the go-ahead to build a mock-up during

the autumn of 1938. This was approved and work then began on the Fw 190 V1 prototype. Armament was initially set to consist of two machine guns and two cannon – a 7.9mm MG 17 with 800 rounds and a 20mm MG 151 with 160 rounds in each wing.

A small retractable ladder was provided on the lower edge of the fuselage on the port side, aft of the wing root, along with a spring-loaded handhold and another step to reach the cockpit. Once aboard, the pilot sat in a semi-reclined seat that was vertically adjustable over a range of 4in. The flight instruments were laid out in what was intended to be a logical way and internal systems received a 24v power supply from a 1000W generator.

The V1 made its first flight on June

1, 1939, but the cockpit was found to become uncomfortably hot within a few minutes and fumes from the engine seeped in. The armed Fw 190 V2 first flew on October 31, 1939, equipped with a FuG VII radio and Revi C/12c gunsight in addition to its weapons.

Following on from the company tradition established by the Stieglitz, Stösser, Weihe and the rest, it was at this time that the Fw 190 was given its 'bird name' – Würger (Shrike). This appeared on company brochures but does not appear to have been more widely adopted.

Overheating problems persisted and the V2 was experimentally fitted with a new 10-bladed cooling fan under its spinner, but this did little to alleviate the issue. Attention was now focused on the

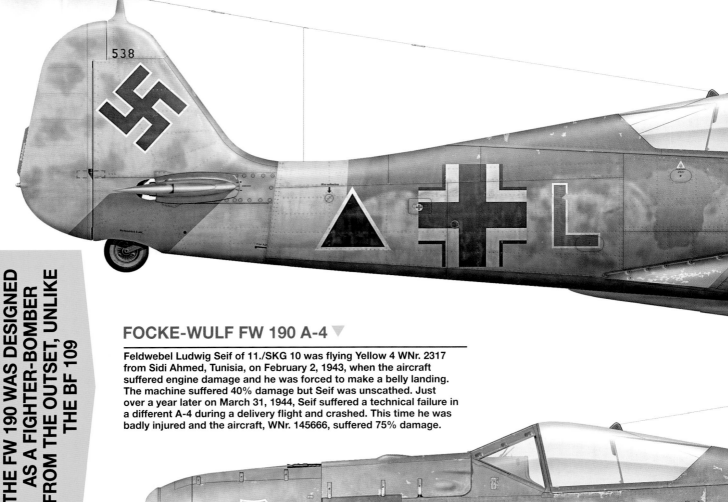

THE FW 190 WAS DESIGNED AS A FIGHTER-BOMBER FROM THE OUTSET, UNLIKE THE BF 109

FOCKE-WULF FW 190 A-4 ▼

Feldwebel Ludwig Seif of 11./SKG 10 was flying Yellow 4 WNr. 2317 from Sidi Ahmed, Tunisia, on February 2, 1943, when the aircraft suffered engine damage and he was forced to make a belly landing. The machine suffered 40% damage but Seif was unscathed. Just over a year later on March 31, 1944, Seif suffered a technical failure in a different A-4 during a delivery flight and crashed. This time he was badly injured and the aircraft, WNr. 145666, suffered 75% damage.

spinner, with BMW arguing that it diverted cool air away from the engine. Focke-Wulf tried it without the Doppelhaube – and discovered that the spinner had actually served to reduce the aircraft's top speed by 12mph, rather than enhancing it.

An order for 40 pre-production Fw 190 A-0 aircraft was placed but the BMW 139 proved to be impossible to keep sufficiently cool. It was therefore replaced by another radial engine that BMW had been working on – the 801. This had a built-in cooling fan and was already proving to be both powerful and reliable.

During testing it was discovered that the Fw 190's canopy was very difficult to open in flight, so a new release mechanism was devised which utilised a 20mm explosive cartridge to push a piston which then punched the canopy rearwards. This would become one of the

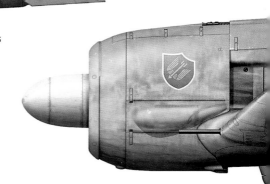

production 190's more distinctive features in combat.

BOMBED UP

It falls outside the scope of this publication to detail all the many fighter versions of the Fw 190 but the earliest examples to be tested with bomb-carrying equipment appear to have been two from a second batch of pre-production aircraft – WNr. 0022, coded SB+IB, and WNr. 0023, coded SB+IC. They flew test flights with either a 500kg bomb or 300 litre drop tank fitted beneath their fuselages up to June 30, 1941. This

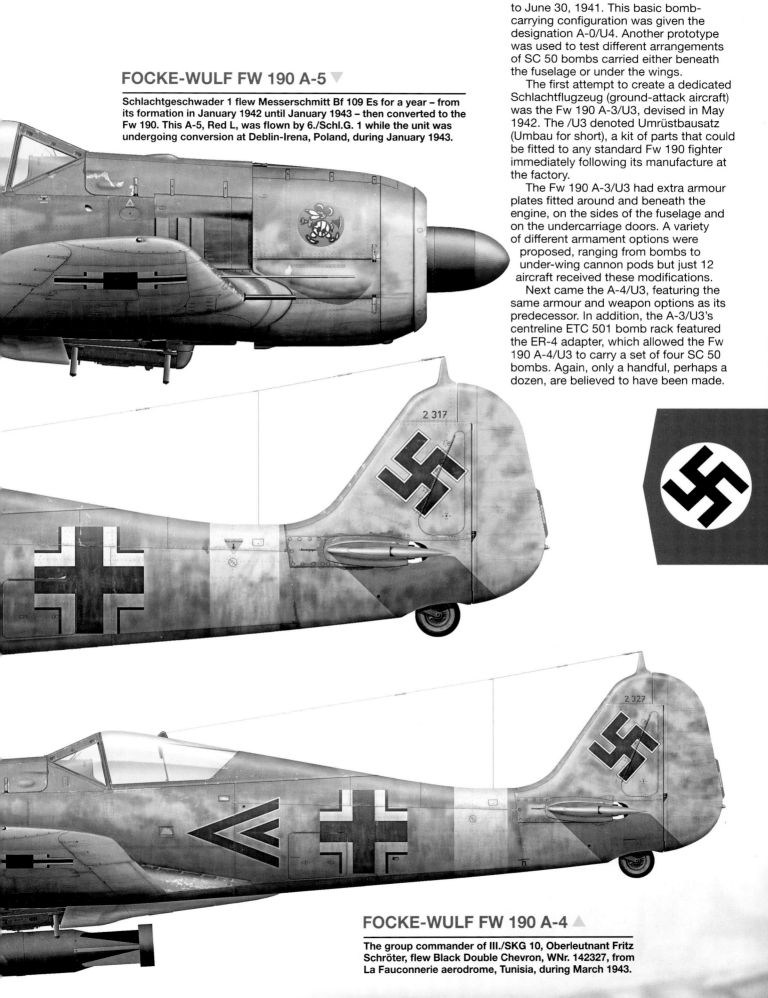

FOCKE-WULF FW 190 A-5 ▼

Schlachtgeschwader 1 flew Messerschmitt Bf 109 Es for a year – from its formation in January 1942 until January 1943 – then converted to the Fw 190. This A-5, Red L, was flown by 6./Schl.G. 1 while the unit was undergoing conversion at Deblin-Irena, Poland, during January 1943.

to June 30, 1941. This basic bomb-carrying configuration was given the designation A-0/U4. Another prototype was used to test different arrangements of SC 50 bombs carried either beneath the fuselage or under the wings.

The first attempt to create a dedicated Schlachtflugzeug (ground-attack aircraft) was the Fw 190 A-3/U3, devised in May 1942. The /U3 denoted Umrüstbausatz (Umbau for short), a kit of parts that could be fitted to any standard Fw 190 fighter immediately following its manufacture at the factory.

The Fw 190 A-3/U3 had extra armour plates fitted around and beneath the engine, on the sides of the fuselage and on the undercarriage doors. A variety of different armament options were proposed, ranging from bombs to under-wing cannon pods but just 12 aircraft received these modifications.

Next came the A-4/U3, featuring the same armour and weapon options as its predecessor. In addition, the A-3/U3's centreline ETC 501 bomb rack featured the ER-4 adapter, which allowed the Fw 190 A-4/U3 to carry a set of four SC 50 bombs. Again, only a handful, perhaps a dozen, are believed to have been made.

FOCKE-WULF FW 190 A-4 ▲

The group commander of III./SKG 10, Oberleutnant Fritz Schröter, flew Black Double Chevron, WNr. 142327, from La Fauconnerie aerodrome, Tunisia, during March 1943.

FOCKE-WULF FW 190 A-5 ▲

White B of 5./SchG 1, Anapa, USSR, as it
appeared during April 1943.

Next came another small-run type, the A-5/U3. This had two ETC 50 racks under each wing and a hefty total armour weight of 794lb. The A-5/U3 was scheduled for limited production in December 1942 with the ultimate goal of using it as the pattern aircraft for the full production Fw 190 F ground-attack aircraft, scheduled to enter production in June 1943.

FW 190 FRIEDRICH

Everything proceeded according to plan until April 1943, when Focke-Wulf changed its mind. The A-4/U3 became officially known as the Fw 190 F-1, while the remaining A-5/U3s became Fw 190 F-2s. A total of up to 270 are believed to have been produced overall.

The template for true mass production of the Friedrich became, instead, the A-5/U17 which was built as the F-3. This was similar to the A-5/U3 but had its outer wing gun positions deleted. Armament was fixed at a pair of MG 17s on the nose and MG 151 20mm cannon in the wing roots. It also had a FuG 16 ZS radio which used army frequencies, allowing the pilot to communicate effectively with the forces on the ground that he was supporting.

Most F-3s left the Arado factory where they were built under licence with a 'field modification' pack or Rüstsatz already fitted. The Fw 190 F-3/R1 had an ETC 501 bomb rack with ER 4 adapter under its fuselage plus two ETC 50s under each wing so it could carry up to eight SC50 50kg bombs. These could be dropped all at once or in pairs using a control device

fitted to the aircraft's cockpit known as the kleine Abwurfelektrik (small electrical release). The extra weight of the bombs caused the aircraft to become unwieldy and top speed dropped dramatically to just 326mph. Therefore most had their nose-mounted machine guns removed for bombing missions.

Other modification packs were planned for the F-3 but few saw action. The F-3/R2 would have seen the aircraft fitted with a podded MK 103 cannon under each wing as a tankbuster but in tests it was found that the MK 103's ammunition was incapable of piercing the Soviet T-34 tank's armour – making it unable to fulfil its primary function.

The R3 was the same as the R2 but with a modified gun fairing and there is thought to have been an R4 but full details of what it might have involved have never been discovered. The R6 was to carry the usual R6 underslung WGr 21 mortar tubes.

F-3/U3, U5 and U14 involved the fitting of specialised racks to enable the aircraft to carry different types of air-launched torpedo.

FOCKE-WULF FW 190 A-5 ▲

Fw 190 fighter-bombers saw heavy use in the Mediterranean Theatre. White H was operated by 5./SchIG 2 from Protville West, Tunisia, during late April 1943.

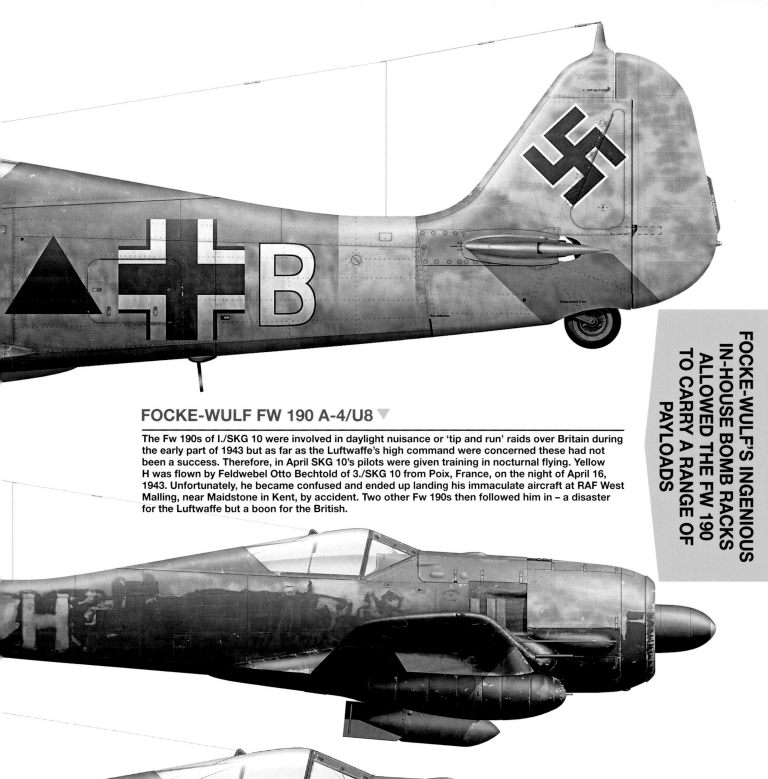

FOCKE-WULF FW 190 A-4/U8 ▼

The Fw 190s of I./SKG 10 were involved in daylight nuisance or 'tip and run' raids over Britain during the early part of 1943 but as far as the Luftwaffe's high command were concerned these had not been a success. Therefore, in April SKG 10's pilots were given training in nocturnal flying. Yellow H was flown by Feldwebel Otto Bechtold of 3./SKG 10 from Poix, France, on the night of April 16, 1943. Unfortunately, he became confused and ended up landing his immaculate aircraft at RAF West Malling, near Maidstone in Kent, by accident. Two other Fw 190s then followed him in – a disaster for the Luftwaffe but a boon for the British.

FOCKE-WULF'S INGENIOUS IN-HOUSE BOMB RACKS ALLOWED THE FW 190 TO CARRY A RANGE OF PAYLOADS

FOCKE-WULF FW 190 A-5 ▼

Leutnant Werner Zirus flew Yellow E with 3./SchlG 2 while based at Milis, Sardinia, during July 1943. Zirus survived the war and went to work as a school teacher. He died on September 8, 2015.

Most of the 432 F-3s produced were built between April and December 1943. Production then dropped to a trickle but continued until the last five were built during March 1944. The first units to receive them were I./SKG 10 in France, I./SG 1 and II./SG 1 in Russia and II./SG 2 in Sicily.

With in-service experience in hand, Focke-Wulf set about working on the next Friedrich, the F-4, which was essentially an F-3 with a refined release system which allowed bombs to be dropped one at a time. However, with the Fw 190 A-8 now in prospect the A-5 airframe on which the F-4 was to be based was becoming increasingly outdated.

LATER FRIEDRICHS

Therefore, the F-4 was cancelled before it could enter even the prototype stage and a revised version was designed based on the A-8, to be known as the F-8. This had the same armament as the A-8 but without the outer wing positions. The F-8 also differed from the A-8 in having a modified injector on its compressor which gave enhanced performance during low-level flying for several minutes.

A handful of conversions and upgrades had been made available for previous Friedrichs but the vast and unprecedented scale of F-8 production – almost on a par with A-8 production – meant the type had a wide range of kits added and modifications made to it.

There were more F-8s than there was fuel to fly them and many ended up as testbeds for armament configurations, unusual anti-tank weapons, rockets and

missiles. They were also used for Mistel combinations detailed elsewhere in this publication.

The G series outlined below was similarly upgraded to G-8 standard with the introduction of the A-8 but after only a small production run it was abandoned in favour of the first F-8 Umrüstbausatz modification – the F-8/U1.

This saw the F-8 fitted with a pair of ETC 503 bomb racks, one under each wing, enabling it to carry a pair of sizeable SC250 250kg bombs, with the centre-mounted ETC 501 for a drop tank. This could also, however, be used for a single SC500 bomb but fitting one exceeded the Fw 190's maximum weight limit and dramatically reduced performance.

FOCKE-WULF FW 190 A-5 ▼

A mountain guide and ski instructor from Sonthofen in Allgäu before the war, Feldwebel Josef 'Sepp' Enzensberger was a ground-attack pilot who flew his first mission during October 1942 – a raid on Malta. Having been injured during a forced landing in Tunisia on February 20, 1943, he then made a second forced landing on March 8, 1943. This was his aircraft, Black Chevron Bar, while he was serving with Stab I./SchlG 2 at Brindisi, Italy, during May 1943. He survived the war only to die in a motorcycle accident on September 6, 1975.

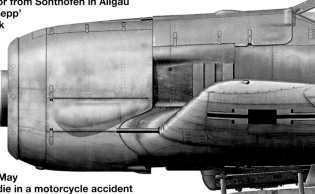

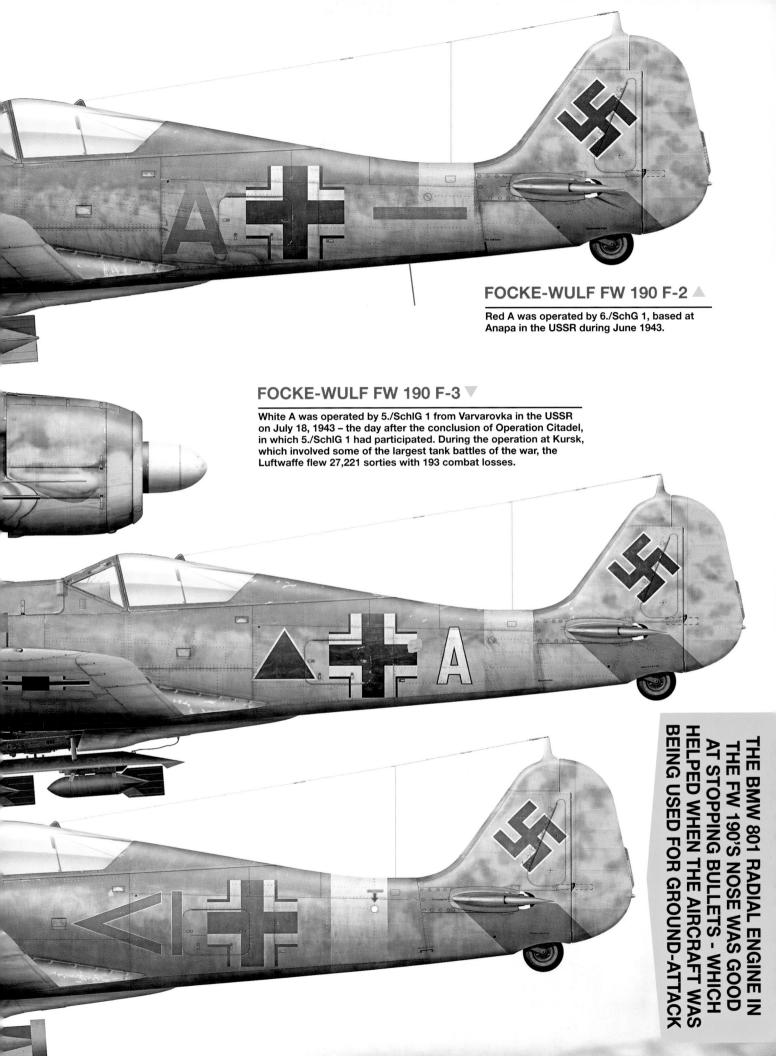

FOCKE-WULF FW 190 F-2 ▲

Red A was operated by 6./SchG 1, based at Anapa in the USSR during June 1943.

FOCKE-WULF FW 190 F-3 ▼

White A was operated by 5./SchIG 1 from Varvarovka in the USSR on July 18, 1943 – the day after the conclusion of Operation Citadel, in which 5./SchIG 1 had participated. During the operation at Kursk, which involved some of the largest tank battles of the war, the Luftwaffe flew 27,221 sorties with 193 combat losses.

THE BMW 801 RADIAL ENGINE IN THE FW 190'S NOSE WAS GOOD AT STOPPING BULLETS - WHICH HELPED WHEN THE AIRCRAFT WAS BEING USED FOR GROUND-ATTACK

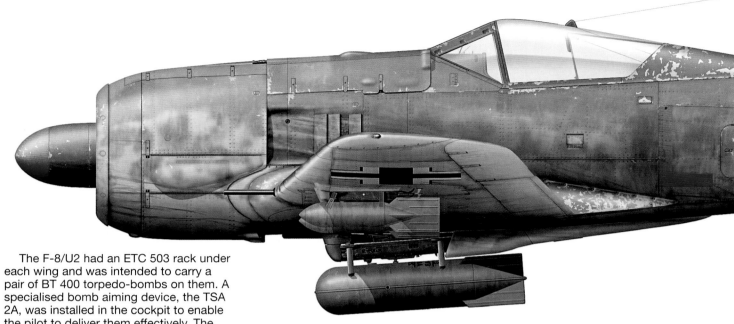

The F-8/U2 had an ETC 503 rack under each wing and was intended to carry a pair of BT 400 torpedo-bombs on them. A specialised bomb aiming device, the TSA 2A, was installed in the cockpit to enable the pilot to deliver them effectively. The aircraft's only other armament was to be the cowling-mounted MG 131 machine guns. Test conversions were made but the U2 never entered full scale production.

The U3 was another torpedo carrying type, this time intended to carry a much larger weapon. It never entered service either. Only one U4 was built, a night version of the F-8 with autopilot and improved electrical systems, and the U5 was similarly an upgrade of electrics only.

In addition to the Umbau conversions, there were seven Rüstsatz field modification kits – R1 was the form in which most F-8s were produced, with a pair of ETC 50 or 71 racks under each wing. R2 saw a pair of 30mm MK 108 cannon fitted in the outer wing positions but only two aircraft were modified this way, by Dornier.

In contrast, up to 60 machines were modified with R3, which had a 30mm MK 103 cannon slung under each wing.

It is possible that some R13s were made, a night ground-attack type with shields to mask engine exhausts from both the pilot and the enemy, and a small number of aircraft modified to R14, with a torpedo rack entered service with 11./KG 200.

This last modification involved substantial changes to the F-8. The usual tail was replaced with the much larger item used on the Ta 152, the tailwheel was lengthened significantly to provide enough space for the underslung torpedo and the BMW 801 TS engine was used in place of the 801D-2. Armament was just two MG 151 cannon, one in each wing root.

F-8/R15 was effectively the F-8/U3 renamed and the R16 was developed from the U2 and only a handful entered service.

Overall, an incredible 3614 Fw 190 F-8s were built, 2264 of them by Arado and 1350 by Norddeutsche Dornier.

FINAL FRIEDRICHS

The development of the Fw 190F did not end here, however. The F-9, powered by the BMW 801 TS, was a ground-attack variant of the A-9 with two cowling-mounted MG 131 machine guns and two MG 151s in the wing roots. It had the usual fitment of an ETC 501 centreline rack, two ETC 50s under each wing and a FuG 16 ZS radio set to enable communication with units on the ground.

It also featured the bulged canopy fitted to late-built A-8s and A-9s.

Production began in January 1945 and it is estimated that some 400 were built, though exact figures are unknown. There were five Rüstsatze – R1 switching the ETC 50 racks for ETC 71s and R13, R14, R15 and R16 matching those of the F-8.

The Fw 190 F-10 was to have been the ground-attack version of the A-10 but this was never built. Focke-Wulf then jumped over the numbers 11-14 and began work, at the end of 1944, on the F-15. This was similar to the F-9 but had larger wheels. The main wheels were 740 x 210mm (up from 700 x 175mm) and the tail wheel was 380 x 150mm (up from 350 x 135mm).

The F-15, too was abandoned before it ever reached production, in favour of an improved version of the design, the F-16. This was to be fitted with the BMW 801 TH, an improved radio set and the bigger wheels. The fuselage rack was the advanced ETC 504 and the wing racks were four ETC 71s or a pair of ETC 503s.

FOCKE-WULF FW 190 F-3 ▲

Hermann Buchner, who had previously flown a Bf 109 with 8./SchlG 1, was flying a Fw 190 designated Red L with 6./SchlG 1 from Charkov-Rogan in the USSR on August 27, 1943 – his 300th combat mission of the war.

FOCKE-WULF FW 190 A-3/U3 ▲

This aircraft, Black 6, was flown by 14.(Jabo)/JG 5 from Petsamo in Finland during September 1943.

FOCKE-WULF FW 190 F-3 ◄

Having flown more than 800 combat missions, around 600 of them in Ju 87s, Hauptmann Alexander Gläser converted to the Fw 190 during early 1944. This was his aircraft, Black Double Chevron, when he assumed command of II./SG 77 at Prokurov in the USSR during March 1944. Overall, Gläser flew 1123 combat missions and survived the war. He died on September 13, 2003, aged 89.

DESPITE THE FLEXIBILITY OFFERED BY THE BASIC A-SERIES AIRFRAME, FOCKE-WULF WENT ON TO BUILD NUMEROUS DEDICATED GROUND-ATTACK VERSIONS IN THE F AND G SERIES

FOCKE-WULF FW 190

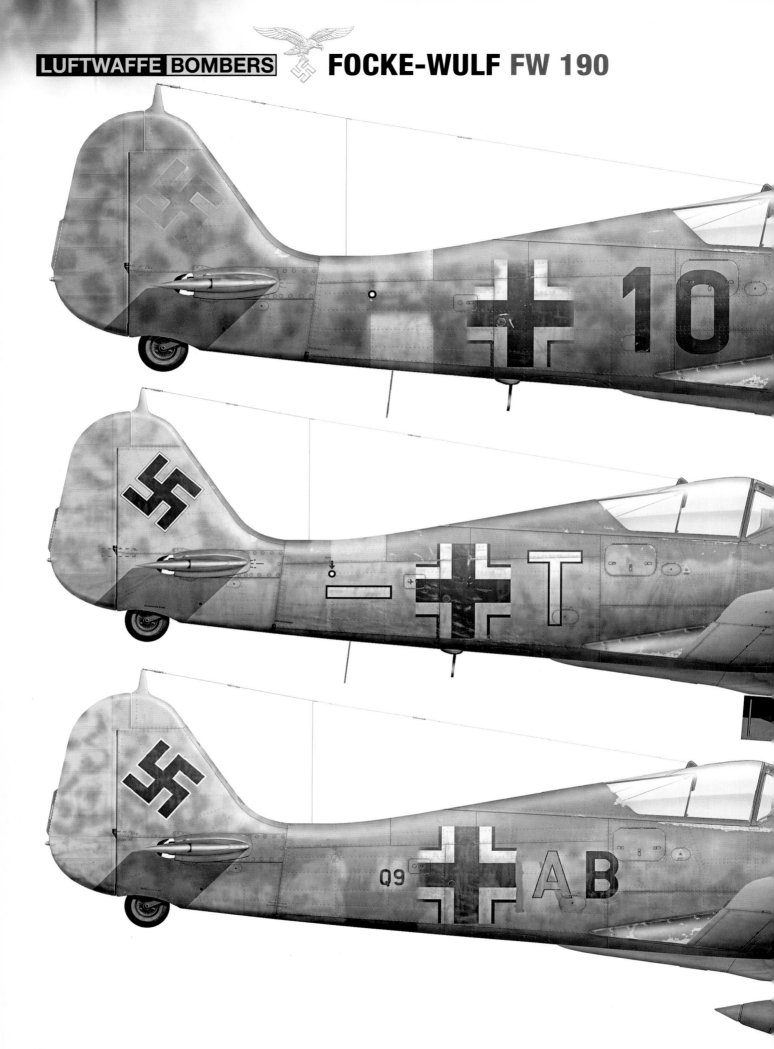

FOCKE-WULF FW 190 F-8 ▼

Black 10 was operated by 2./SG 4 from Rieti, north-east of Rome, Italy, during heavy fighting in May 1944. Rome itself fell to the Allies on June 5, 1944.

Two prototypes were built but the war ended before production could begin.

Finally, and perhaps incredibly, an F-17 was also planned. This was to have the larger tail of the Ta 152 and a BMW 801 TS or TH engine. Production was optimistically scheduled for August 1945.

More than 4000 Fw 190 Fs were built and the majority of them served with units operating on the Eastern Front.

FW 190 GUSTAV

While the Fw 190 F ground-attack aircraft was under development during the autumn of 1942, Focke-Wulf also worked on a long-range fighter model that it called 'Jagdbomber grosser Reichweite' (literally fighter-bomber long range), Jabo-Rei for short, which was based on the earlier A-4/U8, which had a centreline ETC 501 bomb rack but also had all armament removed except for the MG 151 cannon in the wing roots.

The deletion of any nose-mounted weapons allowed for the installation of an additional oil tank to improve the endurance of the aircraft's BMW 801D-2 engine.

A critical factor in the Fw 190 G's design was the ability to carry a drop tank under each wing and since Focke-Wulf did not have the appropriate racks to enable this, it bought in faired racks from Weserflug that had been designed for use on the Ju 87 Stuka – known as the VTr. Ju 87.

While they certainly did the job, these racks reduced the aircraft's speed to an appalling 298mph. Two examples of the A-4/U8 were flown, the first on October 19, 1942, and the second on January 8, 1943, before the type was redesignated the Fw 190 G-1.

A different, fairing-less, wing rack was then trialled in the hope of reducing

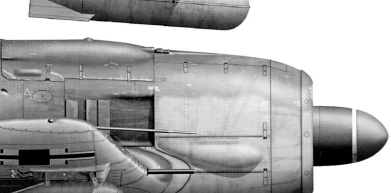

FOCKE-WULF FW 190 F-8 ▲

4./SG 2's White T was based at Zilistea, Romania, during June 1944. The unit had been withdrawn there a month earlier having suffered substantial losses on the Eastern Front.

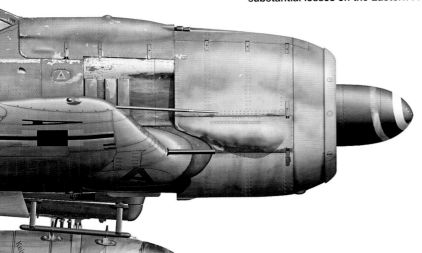

FOCKE-WULF FW 190 F-8 ◄

The second aircraft flown by Hauptmann Fritz Schröter in this chapter is Q9+AB, which he flew with Stab I./SG 5, during August 1944, based at Utti in Finland. The unit only remained at Utti for 10 days before being moved to Estonia on August 13.

THE G-SERIES DIFFERED FROM THE F MAINLY IN HAVING THE PLUMBING NECESSARY FOR UNDER-WING DROP TANKS

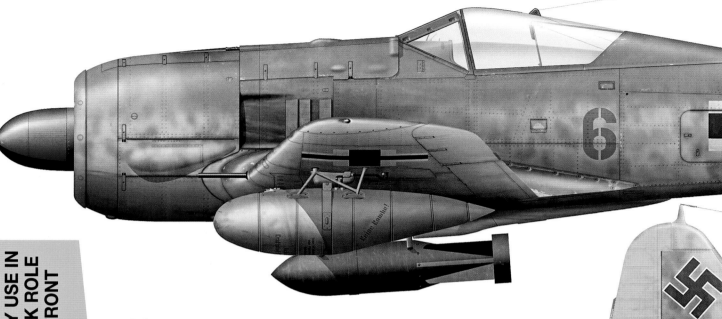

THE FW 190 SAW PARTICULARLY HEAVY USE IN THE GROUND-ATTACK ROLE ON THE EASTERN FRONT

FOCKE-WULF FW 190 G-3 ▲

Feldwebel Otto Putz of 8./KG 51 flew Red 6 from Roye-Amy in France on August 19, 1944 – the day Paris was liberated. Just under three weeks later Roye-Amy was in American hands and redesignated A-73 Roye/Amy Airfield.

FOCKE-WULF FW 190 F-8 ▶

Chevron E of Stab II./SG 4, based at Tilit, Latvia, in July 1944. The unit had been moved there following a rest in northern Italy at the beginning of the month in order to support Army Groups North and Centre in opposing the huge Soviet summer and autumn offensives.

FOCKE-WULF FW 190 F-8 ▲

Famous Ju 87 ground-attack specialist Oberstleutnant Hans-Ulrich Rudel joined SG 2 on September 1, 1944, and Black Chevron and Bar was his aircraft 22 days later while the unit was stationed at Görgenyoroszfalu in Romania. Rudel was appointed to lead the unit on October 1.

FOCKE-WULF FW 190 F-8 ▶

Black Chevron Green 2 was flown by pilots of Stab I./SG 2 from Papa, western Hungary, during January 1945.

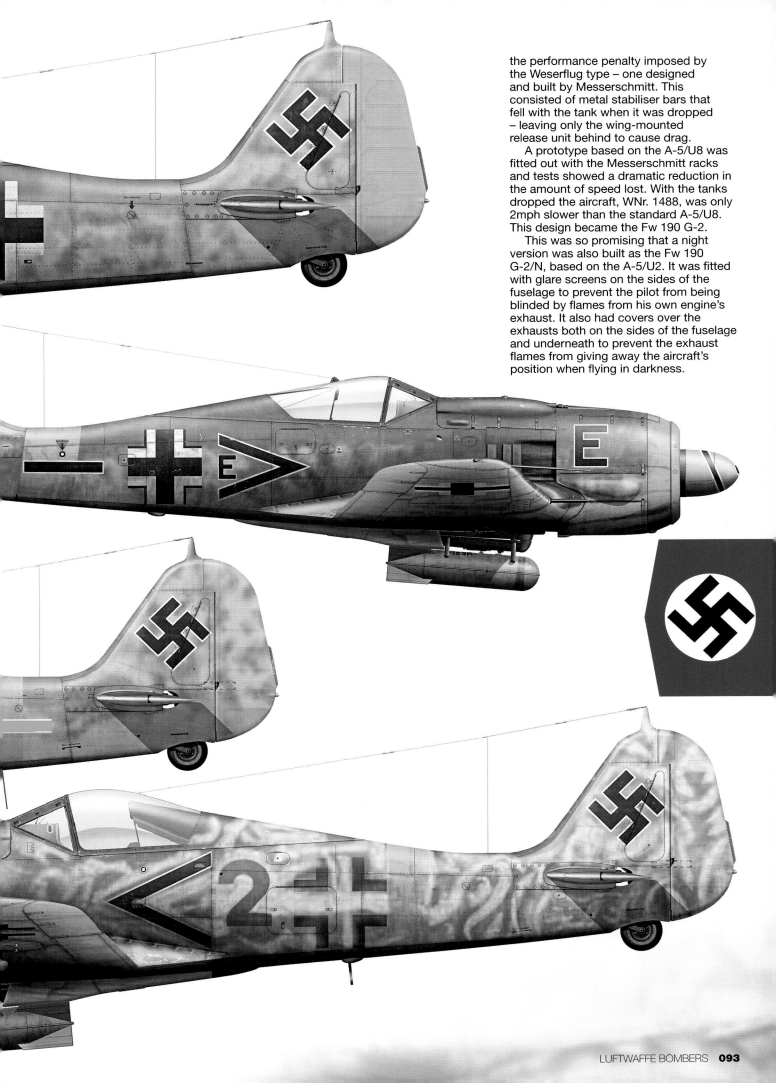

the performance penalty imposed by the Weserflug type – one designed and built by Messerschmitt. This consisted of metal stabiliser bars that fell with the tank when it was dropped – leaving only the wing-mounted release unit behind to cause drag.

A prototype based on the A-5/U8 was fitted out with the Messerschmitt racks and tests showed a dramatic reduction in the amount of speed lost. With the tanks dropped the aircraft, WNr. 1488, was only 2mph slower than the standard A-5/U8. This design became the Fw 190 G-2.

This was so promising that a night version was also built as the Fw 190 G-2/N, based on the A-5/U2. It was fitted with glare screens on the sides of the fuselage to prevent the pilot from being blinded by flames from his own engine's exhaust. It also had covers over the exhausts both on the sides of the fuselage and underneath to prevent the exhaust flames from giving away the aircraft's position when flying in darkness.

FOCKE-WULF FW 190

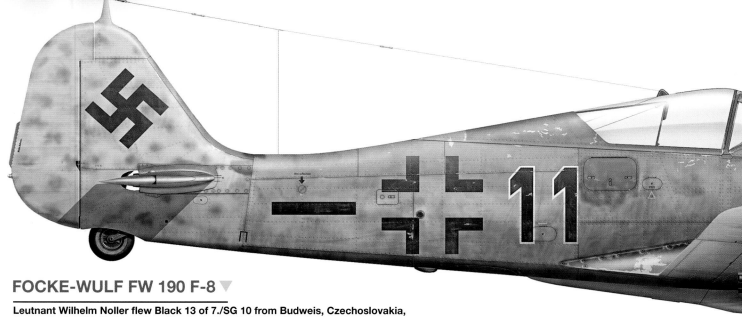

FOCKE-WULF FW 190 F-8 ▼

Leutnant Wilhelm Noller flew Black 13 of 7./SG 10 from Budweis, Czechoslovakia, during April 1945. Noller enlisted in the Luftwaffe in October 1939 and trained as a pilot from March to December 1940. He then trained as a dive-bomber pilot and was posted to the Eastern Front. After completing 1000 missions, in June 1944, he was able to attend officer school and become a leutnant. After a spell as an instructor, he joined 7./SG 10 in February 1945. Wounded in action on April 16, 1945, he was hospitalised in Prague, where he was captured by the Soviets. On June 2, while being transferred by train to Russia, he jumped off and managed to escape – making his way back to Germany. He survived the war and died in 2011.

THE WIDE-TRACK UNDERCARRIAGE OF THE FW 190 CERTAINLY HELPED WHEN IT CAME TO TAKING OFF WITH LARGE BOMB LOADS

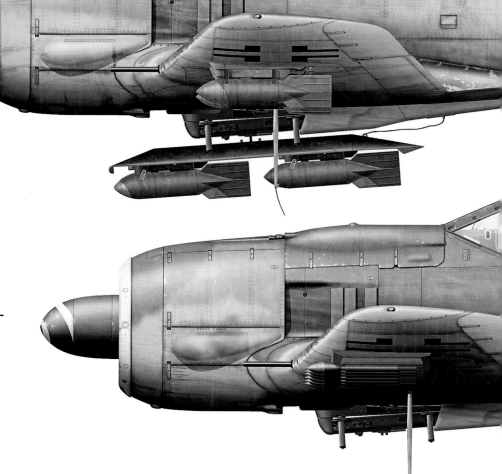

FOCKE-WULF FW 190 F-9 ▶

Born in New York City, Helmut Wenk moved to southern Germany in his youth. During the Defence of the Reich campaign, he flew Yellow 7 with III./SG 10, based at Prerau in Slovakia, during April 1945. Despite being a ground-attack pilot, he shot down a Soviet La-5 on April 27.

FOCKE-WULF FW 190 F-8 ◀

During March 1945, some of SG 77's Fw 190s were fitted with Panzerblitz 80mm anti-tank rockets on racks under their outboard wings. Among those aircraft was Black 11 of 5./SG 77, depicted here as it appeared at the Focke-Wulf factory airfield at Cottbus, Germany. Cottbus became a front line base in January 1945 as the Soviets advanced. It finally fell to the Russians on April 23, 1945.

The G-2 entered production and the first examples were allocated to SKG 10 in France in June 1943. However, even though the installation of the Messerschmitt rack had been a resounding success, Focke-Wulf still felt that there was room for improvement and developed its own purpose-built rack – which resulted in an 11mph loss of speed with only the racks fitted.

Nevertheless, the G-3 entered production with its Focke-Wulf fittings and was also built in a night version similar to the G-2/N. Conversions to G-3/U3, U5 and U14 were all devised to allow the G-3 to carry torpedoes. The G-3/R1 gave the aircraft the same armament as the A-6/R1 – a pair of podded MG 151/20 cannon under each wing, four in total.

Perhaps even more extreme, the G-3/R5 reinstated the nose-mounted machine guns, MG 131s and added a pair of ETC 71 racks under each wing to create an aircraft that was more like a Fw 190 F than a G.

All 550 G-3s were built by Focke-Wulf and the type was operated by SKG 10, SG 4 and SG 10.

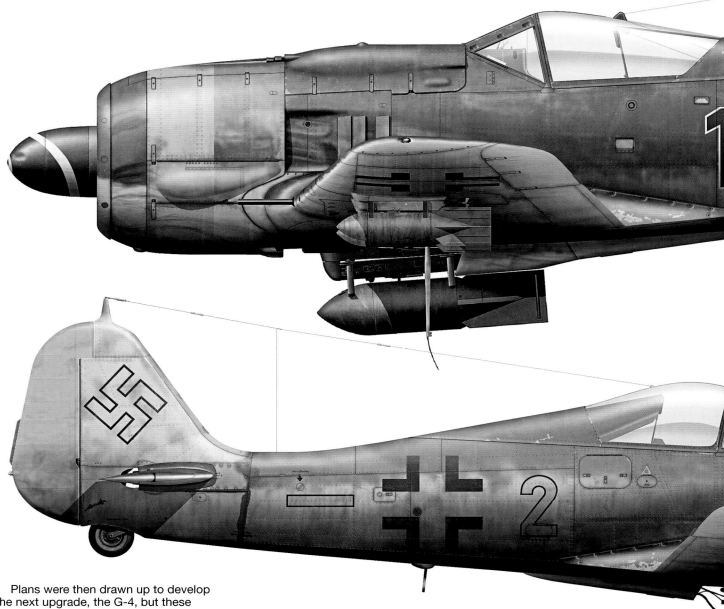

Plans were then drawn up to develop the next upgrade, the G-4, but these were dropped when it became clear that a major production drive would be made centred on the new A-8.

The G-8 was to have the familiar ETC 501 centreline bomb rack plus an ETC 503 rack beneath each wing for the 300 litre drop tanks. The advanced ETC 503 only caused a speed loss of 4mph – an acceptable compromise. As with previous Gustavs, armament was reduced to the wing-root MG 151s and the F-8's bulged canopy was also fitted. Focke-Wulf built all 146 G-8s as G-8/R5s in March and April 1944. These had a pair of ETC 50 or 71 racks under each wing.

Some Fw 190 Gs were field modified to carry very large payloads of 1000kg, 1600kg or even 1800kg. This was managed by modifying the landing gear oleo struts and using reinforced tyres.

Experiments were carried out to fit the Fw 190 G with water-methanol injection to boost performance and a night time version, the G-8/N, got as far as tests with

FOCKE-WULF FW 190 F-8 ▼

With the Soviets closing in, on April 26, 1945, Major Erhard Jähnert of Stab III./SG 3 flew Black A away from the doomed Courland Pocket with his unit in order to surrender to the British at Flensburg in Germany. He died in 2006.

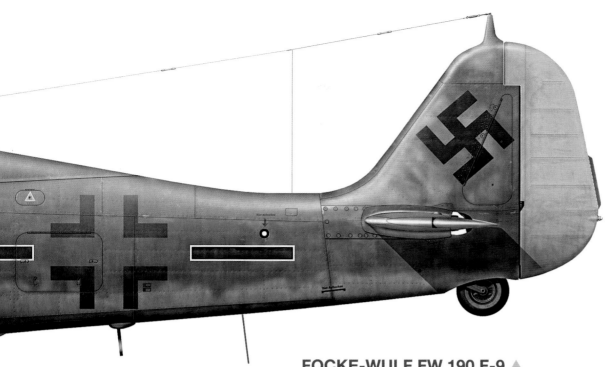

FOCKE-WULF FW 190 F-9 ▲

Oberfeldwebel Erich Axthammer of Stab II./SG 10 flew Black 1 Bar from Budweis in Czechoslovakia during late April 1945. Axthammer survived the war and served with the Bundeswehr from October 1958 to March 31, 1973. He died on December 21, 2015.

FOCKE-WULF FW 190 F-8 ◄

Yellow 2, WNr. 586875 was operated by 6./SG 10 from Hörsching in Austria during late April 1945.

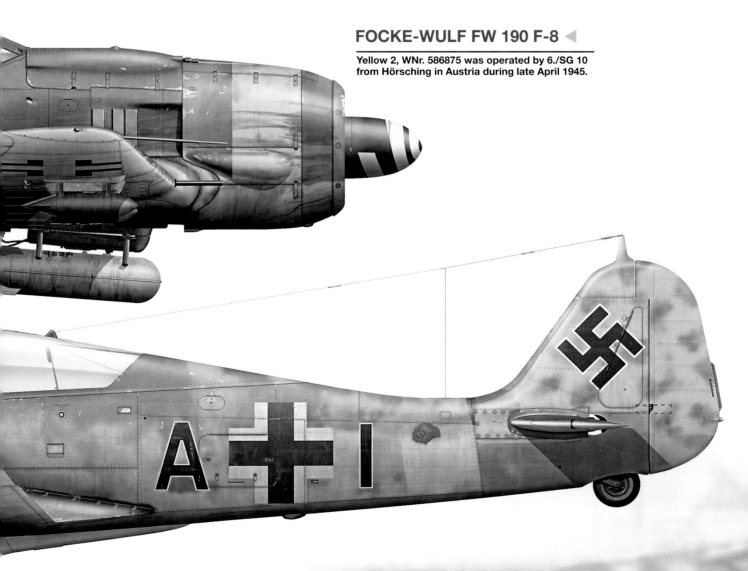

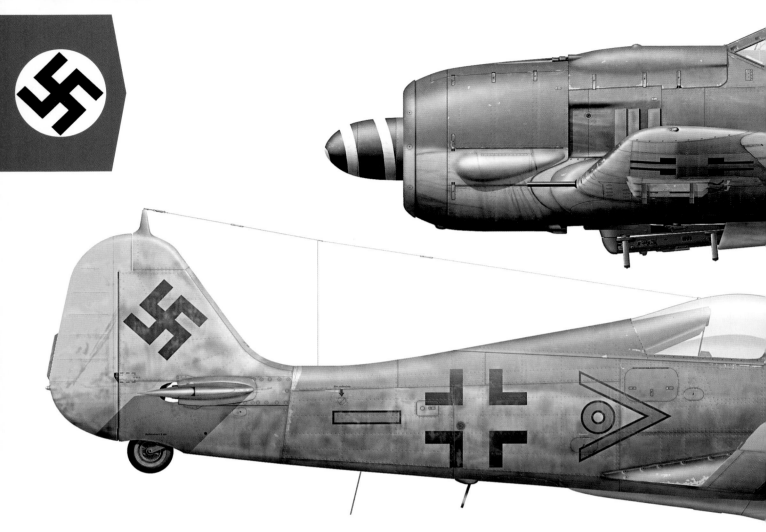

FOCKE-WULF FW 190 F-9 ▲

Green Chevron and Dot, WNr. 440401 of Stab II./SG 10, as it was left at Wels in Austria on the last day of the war – May 8, 1945.

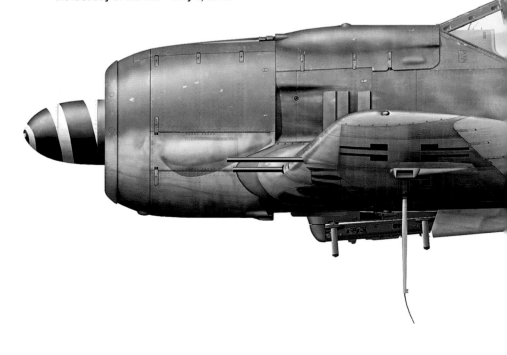

a prototype but when production of the G-8/R5 drew to a premature conclusion in April 1944, the Gustav was wound up in favour of further Fw 190 F developments. G-9 and G-10 variants had been pencilled in but these were scrapped.

Around 1300 Fw 190 Gs of all types had been built by the end of the war, though some of these were composites made using, for example, the undamaged wings from one wrecked aircraft and the undamaged fuselage of another. As with the Fw 190 F, most of these served on the Eastern Front.

The Fw 190's many fighter-bomber variants appear to have been something of an embarrassment to Reichsmarschall Hermann Göring who believed that the Luftwaffe ought to be operating a specialised fast bomber instead. However, all efforts to design and build such an aircraft ultimately met with failure and the sturdy Fw 190 soldiered on until the end of the war. It played a key role in providing close air support during the last stages of the war – particularly during the Battle of Berlin in late April and early May 1945. ●

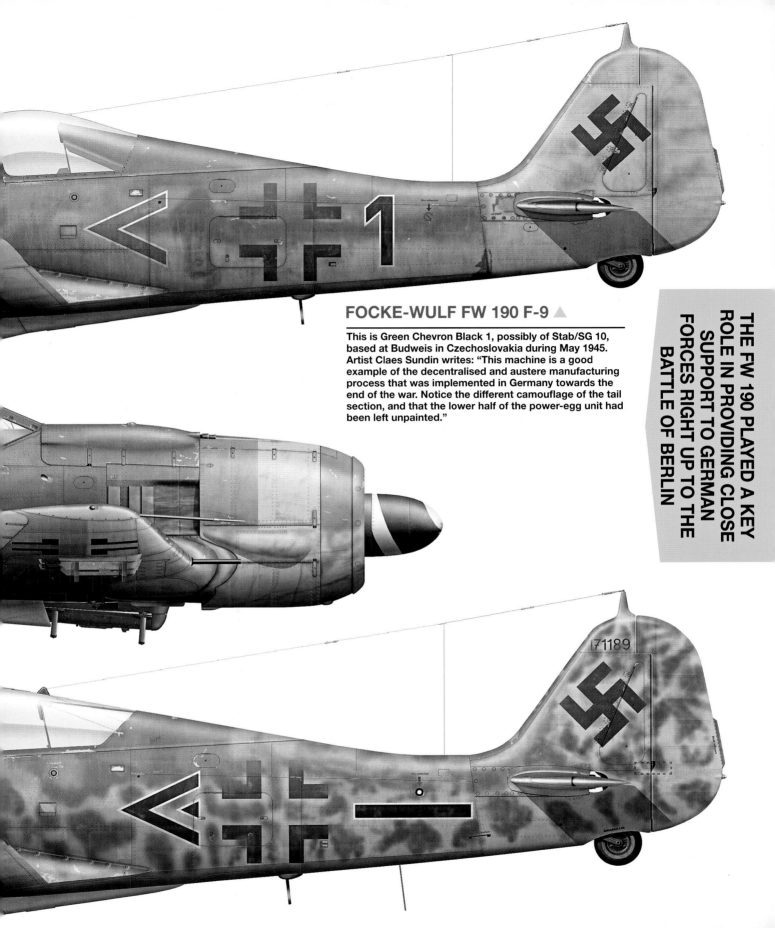

FOCKE-WULF FW 190 F-9 ▲

This is Green Chevron Black 1, possibly of Stab/SG 10, based at Budweis in Czechoslovakia during May 1945. Artist Claes Sundin writes: "This machine is a good example of the decentralised and austere manufacturing process that was implemented in Germany towards the end of the war. Notice the different camouflage of the tail section, and that the lower half of the power-egg unit had been left unpainted."

THE FW 190 PLAYED A KEY ROLE IN PROVIDING CLOSE SUPPORT TO GERMAN FORCES RIGHT UP TO THE BATTLE OF BERLIN

FOCKE-WULF FW 190 A-8 ▲

Major Karl Kessel, commander of II./SG 2 flew Double Black Chevron from Kummer, north of Prague, Czechoslovakia, on May 8, 1945. German forces – survivors of Army Group Centre – trapped in the centre of Prague continued to resist Soviet forces until May 11 – three days after Germany's unconditional surrender. Some individual units reportedly held out for longer still.

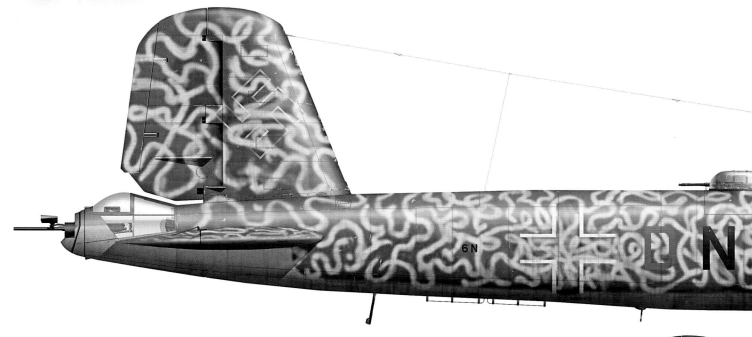

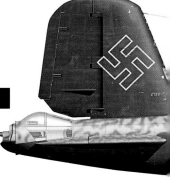

HEINKEL HE 177

Designed to incorporate all the very latest developments in aviation technology, the Heinkel He 177 should have provided the Luftwaffe with a fast and modern heavy bomber. Instead, it became a source of endless difficulties which had enormous ramifications for both the German air force and Heinkel itself.

The RLM issued a specification for a Langstrecken-Grossbomber or 'long-range heavy bomber' in 1935 and only two firms were invited to tender designs – Dornier and Junkers. Their proposals, the Do 19 and Ju 89, were approved for prototype construction but neither was particularly fast and each had at least one particularly unappealing design flaw. The Do 19 was to have heavy two-man turrets, the weight of which hampered its already weak performance, and the Ju 89 suffered from longitudinal instability.

By 1936 it was evident that other companies felt far better performance could be achieved and on June 3 that year a second heavy bomber specification was issued with stringent requirements, particularly with regard to speed, that superseded those of the Langstrecken-Grossbomber.

The new Fernbomber or 'long-range bomber' would have to be able to carry 500kg of bombs 5000km with a top speed of 500kph at an altitude of 5500m. Neither Langstrecken-Grossbomber design came close

HEINKEL HE 177 A-5 ▼

Unusually, the bomb aimer of 6N+DN, WNr. 550131, Hauptmann Hans Schacke, was the highest ranking officer and therefore Staffelkapitän of 5./KG 100. The pilot was Oberfeldwebel Willy Niederstadt. The aircraft is pictured as it appeared at Aalborg-West in Denmark during late February 1944. Although the crews of II./KG 100 had been trained to launch the Hs 293 during anti-shipping operations, they had few opportunities to do so before fuel shortages and operational conditions made this impossible.

HEINKEL HE 177 A-3 ▼

Sporting night camouflage NF+GB of FFS(B) 18, is seen here as it looked at Burg-bei-Magdeburg in Germany during March 1944.

on range or speed, although each could carry a heavier bomb load.

The firms included in this competition were Junkers, Hamburger Flugzeugbau, Bayerische Flugzeugwerke (soon to be Messerschmitt), Henschel and Heinkel.

All of the competitors offered four-engined bomber designs but Heinkel's P 1041 had its four 1100hp DB 601 engines linked in pairs as two DB 606s. The two DB 601s were connected via a single gearing system to a single propeller

shaft and the DB 606 combination ought in theory to have been capable of more than 2000hp each.

Two engines running together in a confined space generated a lot of heat, but rather than fit drag-inducing radiators, Heinkel's designers proposed an evaporative cooling system. The water/antifreeze coolant was pressurised so that it could remain liquid above its usual boiling point. Fully heated, it was

then ducted away and depressurised, becoming steam. This was condensed by running it through pipes in the wing where it was exposed to the cold air outside the aircraft. Liquid again, it was fed right back into the engine to repeat the process.

And the innovation didn't end there. In order to reduce wing thickness, each of the two large main undercarriage wheels on either side was mounted on a separate leg – one retracting towards the

HEINKEL HE 177 A-3 ▼

Stab./KG 100 operated 6N+CK from Châteaudun in France during March to April 1944. The aircraft is believed to have participated in Operation Steinbock – the final strategic air offensive by the German bomber arm during the Second World War. Known later as the 'Baby Blitz', it began in January 1944 and ended in May 1944, targeting the Greater London area. More than 470 aircraft were assembled for the offensive but 329 had been lost by the end of the operation and little had been achieved. KG 100 had only 11 operational aircraft left, having had 21 on March 20.

HEINKEL HE 177

HEINKEL HE 177 A-5 ▼

Having flown anti-shipping operations with the Hs 293 from Bordeux-Mérignac, France, during June 1944, as it appears here, F8+KP of 6./KG 40 was captured by the French during the latter half of August 1944 at Toulouse-Blagnac. They painted over its German markings with invasion stripes and French insignia. It was delivered to the British in September 1944 who then added their own markings and used the aircraft for various tests before scrapping it.

fuselage and one towards the outer wing when the undercarriage was raised after take-off. The aircraft would be so fast that defensive armament could be light – just one manned MG 131 machine gun in each of the nose, tail, upper and lower fuselage positions.

The RLM approved and Heinkel received its development contract. The first P 1041 mock-up was inspected by RLM representatives at Heinkel's Rostock-Marienehe headquarters on August 6, 1937. Changes were requested – better visibility for the crew, better positioning of the gun turrets and a clearer layout of cockpit instrumentation – but these issues were quickly resolved and the design was approved for production on November 11, 1937, as the He 177.

At this point, the Luftwaffe's plans were firmly based on fighting a limited ground war with support from dive-bombers and close-support aircraft. Heinkel was told that his heavy bomber would have to be capable of dive-bombing and an order for six He 177 prototypes was placed with Heinkel in October 1938 on the condition that it would be able to do just that.

On November 19, 1938, Ernst Heinkel proposed that the second and third prototypes of the He 177 should be built as normal four-engined aircraft with four single Jumo 211s, but the General Staff denied permission for this on the basis that "the efficiency of the He 177 in dive-bombing depends upon the use of only two power units. The normal four-engined plane cannot be used as a dive-bomber. A development in that direction is consequently ruled out."

On February 24, 1939, the number of He 177 prototypes on order was increased to 12 and on July 6 a further order for 20 pre-production aircraft was placed. In August, Heinkel received a full production order for 800 aircraft, to be fulfilled by April 1943. Work on building the He 177 prototypes was now well under way.

In September 1939 it was decided that the He 177's defensive gun positions should be swapped for drag-reducing remotely-controlled ones except the one in the nose. And by now it was all too apparent to Heinkel that fitting DB 606s to

the He 177 was going to cause serious problems.

Tests show that the cooling system was ineffective and the cramped housing of the DB 606s meant their coiled up pipes tended to leak at the joints, filling the nacelles with flammable liquids. At high altitudes, the engine's oil tended to foam up, reducing its lubricating properties and causing the engine con rod bearings to disintegrate. When the rod eventually tore through the engine case, oil flooded out onto the hot exhaust – starting the fire.

Several prototypes were lost to crashes and production of the He 177 A-1 commenced in December 1941 without the problems having been resolved. The aircraft quickly developed a reputation as a death trap just waiting to burst into flames.

A long-range reconnaissance version, the A-2, was proposed but this never came to fruition and the next major production version of the He 177 was the A-3. This was powered by the DB 610 – a pair of linked DB 605s with many of the problems that had plagued the DB 606 installation of the A-1 ironed out. The A-3 also had a lengthened fuselage, greater bomb load capacity, an extra upper turret housing an MG 131, structural strengthening and an enlarged tail fin and rudder.

Production of the A-3, without the fuselage extension, began in November 1942 and continued to July 1943. The extended A-3 was then in production from August 1943 to June 1944. More than 600 examples were built during this time.

The A-4 was an unbuilt high-altitude version and the final variant, the A-5, went into production in December 1943. This was designed for carrying external loads including the Hs 293 missile and LT 50 torpedo. It was based on the A-3 but had shorter undercarriage legs, strengthened wings and a cockpit modified to improve downwards visibility

HEINKEL HE 177 A-5 ▼

Another anti-shipping He 177 from Aalborg-West in Denmark – 6N+GM, WNr. 550047 belonged to 4./KG 100 and this is how it looked in July 1944.

HEINKEL HE 177 A-5 ▼

6N+KM, WNr. 550045 of 4./KG 100, as it appeared at Bordeaux-Mérignac, France, on August 19, 1944 – the day Paris was liberated.

for the crew. The last He 177 A-5 rolled off
the line in August 1944.

Early examples of the He 177 certainly
helped it to earn the nickname 'flaming
coffin' and even by the end of its
production lifespan the He 177 remained
a difficult aircraft to fly and a difficult
aircraft to trust. Given the huge amount of
effort put into its design, development and
production it must rank among German
aviation's wartime greatest failures. ●

HEINKEL HE 177 A-3 ▼

At midday on July 20, 1944, 80 He 177s,
including V4+KL of 3./KG 1 began to take off
in three waves from bases in Germany for
an operation. While they were forming up
above a lake near Rastenburg, two aircraft
developed engine problems and ditched their
bombs before heading back to base. When
the commander of KG 1, Oberstleutnant
Horst von Riesen returned to base after the
mission at 6pm he was told he would be
court marshalled for having his crews drop
bombs on Hitler's headquarters, the Wolf's
Lair at Rastenburg. After anxiously awaiting
the arrival of an officer from the legal branch,
who was to gather evidence against him,
he was eventually told he was 'off the hook'
– the bomb that blew up at the Wolf's Lair
had actually been the July 20 assassination
attempt on Hitler's life.

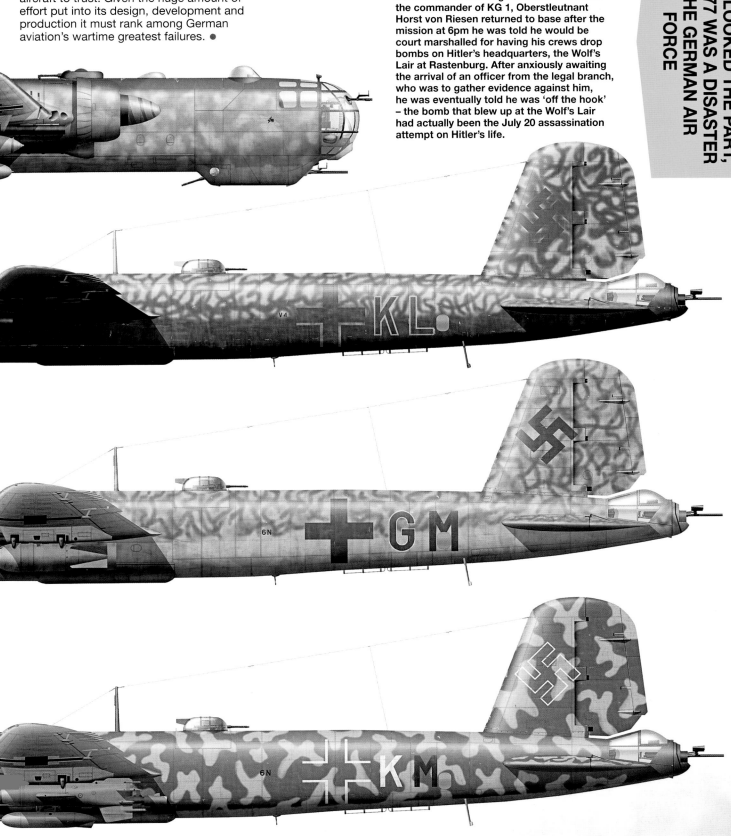

HENSCHEL HS 129

1938-1945

While many of the Luftwaffe's types were adapted for destroying tanks, it only had one dedicated tank-buster – the heavily armed and armoured Henschel Hs 129. Built in relatively small numbers, it nevertheless proved to be a highly effective ground-attack weapon.

T he Hs 123 and Ju 87 had proven effective as dive-bombers attacking static targets but combat experience during the Spanish Civil War from 1936 to 1939 indicated that a dedicated ground-attack aircraft capable of tracking and destroying highly mobile targets such as tanks, armoured fighting vehicles and soft-skinned vehicles would be necessary in future conflicts.

The RLM therefore issued a requirement in April 1937 for a twin-engine aircraft that could be equipped with a 20mm cannon, heavy machine guns

and a bomb load. The recommended powerplant was the 430hp Argus As 410 A-0. No particular specification was given for rear defence but good armour protection for the pilot was deemed essential. The aircraft was also required to be durable and easy to maintain.

Focke-Wulf, Gotha, Hamburger Flugzeugbau (HFB – later Blohm & Voss) and Henschel were all invited to tender but when the deadline for tenders arrived on October 1, 1937, Gotha had failed to make a submission. Focke-Wulf proposed a version of its existing Fw 189

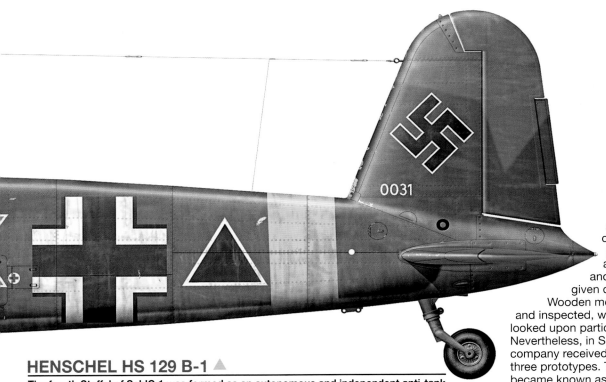

HENSCHEL HS 129 B-1 ▲

The fourth Staffel of SchlG 1 was formed as an autonomous and independent anti-tank unit in January 1942. Initially equipped with Bf 109 Es, it was soon re-equipped with 16 Hs 129 B-1s. Early missions, in May 1942, involved attacking Soviet airfields in Eastern Crimea before moving to support German forces in the Kharkov area. This example, Blue K, was flown by 4.(Pz)/SchlG 1 while it was stationed at Kharkov-Rogan in the USSR during June 1942.

reconnaissance design, a twin-seater, and HFB offered a small asymmetrical design – the P 40 – which appears to have been an entirely new proposition and unrelated to the later asymmetrical Ha 141 reconnaissance machine. It had a wingspan of 12m and a wing area of 27sqm, compared to the Ha 141's 17.45m wingspan and 52.9sqm wing area. What it actually looked like, however, is unknown today.

Henschel also put forward an entirely new design, believed to have been the P 46, but where the others had offered a relatively unusual layout the design that would become the Hs 129 was largely conventional in appearance at first glance. It was smaller than the Fw 189, though somewhat larger than the HFB project, with an unusual triangular fuselage cross-

section. This was apparently intended to offer a smaller target to enemies firing up from the ground, while its flat sides were meant to deflect bullets coming from that direction.

The Henschel design's cockpit was cramped – with the width having been dictated by the broadness of a man's shoulders on average – but both front and rear were heavily armoured. The aircraft's seat back and headrest were to be made from 5mm thick plate, while the windscreen was made from two sheets of bulletproof glass 75mm thick. Beyond the windscreen, the Henschel's nose sloped steeply away, providing excellent visibility forward and downwards. In fact, the cockpit was so short on space that the Revi C/12C gunsight had to be positioned outside the windscreen.

After the initial round of discussions, HFB's proposal was rejected and both Henschel and Focke-Wulf were given development contracts. Wooden mock-ups were built and inspected, with neither being looked upon particularly favourably. Nevertheless, in September 1938 each company received a contract to build three prototypes. The Focke-Wulf project became known as the Fw 189 S while the P 46 became the Hs 129.

Focke-Wulf set about constructing a small new armoured cockpit for the original Fw 189 V1 prototype to create the first Fw 189 S, but Henschel was starting from scratch and initially made slow progress. The Fw 189 S V1 was ready to fly in early 1939 while the Hs 129 V1 lagged several months behind. It was finally completed during the spring but still lacked its As 410 inline engines and propellers from Argus.

These were eventually delivered and the Hs 129 V1 made its first flight on May 26, 1939. Early testing revealed some serious problems, however, particular with regard to pilot visibility. The only way to see out of the aircraft was through thick armoured glass, which meant all-round spatial awareness was compromised. In addition, the Hs 129 lacked power and its handling was found to be only average.

The Fw 189 S had similar difficulties in this regard but was also heavier overall thanks to its twin-boom layout. When the Fw 189 S V1 crashed during testing due

HENSCHEL HS 129 B-1 ▼

Yellow L was operated by 5./SchlG 1, based at Tatsinskaya, USSR, in July 1942. The unit supported the 6th Army during the drive on Stalingrad, although losses during this period were surprisingly light.

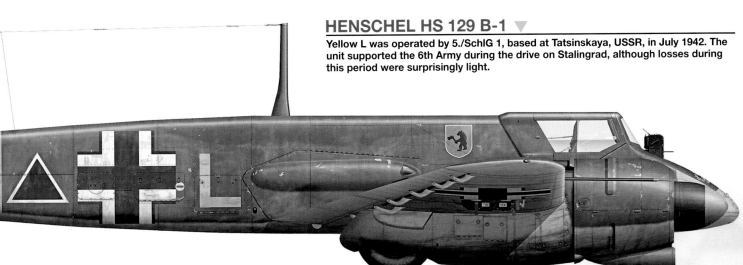

HENSCHEL HS 129

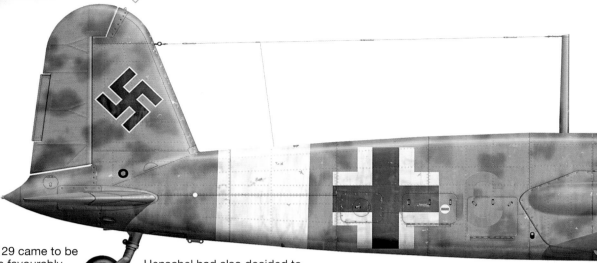

to poor visibility, the Hs 129 came to be regarded somewhat more favourably. Meanwhile, Focke-Wulf set about redesigning the Fw 189 S's cockpit as a single-seater. However, this crash-landed once again on November 8, 1939.

The Hs 129 V2 took to the air for the first time on November 30 but was destroyed after failing to recover from a dive during a test flight on January 5, 1940. The surviving V1 was then joined by the newly constructed V3 on April 2, 1940. By now, the specialists at the Rechlin test centre had come down firmly in favour of the Hs 129. Another decisive factor was its cost – only two-thirds that of the Focke-Wulf contender. The Fw 189 had now been redesignated Fw 189 C but it was now only considered to be a reserve choice.

While the Hs 129 V1 and V3 were still being evaluated, in July 1940 the RLM ordered a series of 20 Hs 129 A-0 pre-production aircraft and Henschel set about constructing them. The first rolled off the production line at the end of the month and made its first test flight on August 1, 1940. A month later, the RLM scaled its order back to just 12 A-0s and cancelled a series of 16 A-1 full production aircraft. The focus was instead shifted to a new version of the Hs 129 which was to have more powerful engines – the B-series.

In early 1941 it was decided that the B-series Hs 129s should be powered by Gnome-Rhone 14M radial engines, which produced 700hp each. This meant that the Henschel production line would not be dependent on German engines which were in high demand elsewhere for fighters and bombers. It was hoped that eventually a more powerful BMW or Argus engine would become available but in the end the Hs 129 was stuck with the 14M.

The early Hs 129 A-0s were re-engined with 14Ms following successful installation of the powerplant – which was significantly larger and heavier than the As 410 – in the Hs 129 V3. It made its first flight in this new configuration on March 19, 1941, and pilots found its performance significantly improved as expected.

During the delays caused by this work,

Henschel had also decided to remodel the aircraft's cockpit. In place of the two-panel windscreen a new single pane of armoured glass was adopted. The side windows were significantly enlarged and the metal plate which previously sat above the pilot's head was replaced by another panel of bulletproof glass. These changes taken together dramatically improved visibility from the pilot's seat and some of the cockpit's engine instruments were moved outside the cockpit to free up more space.

The first fully reconfigured B-0 was finished in August 1941, with the next two being completed in September. The initial batch of 18 had all been produced by early the following year. Work then began on the full production B-1. An order for 250 was placed in October 1941 but in April 1942 this was changed to 250 Hs 129 B-2s with an option to buy up to a further 1000 examples.

The B-2 incorporated a large number of minor detail changes based on early combat experience with the Hs 129: the engine cowlings were altered to improve

HENSCHEL HS 129 B-2 ▶

The German forces in Stalingrad were caught off guard when the Soviets launched a sweeping counter-offensive on November 19, 1942. I./SchG 1 was forced to destroy some of its unserviceable Bf 109 E-7s before retreating while the Hs 129s of II./SchG 1 were thrown into the front line, suffering heavy casualties before also being compelled to withdraw as the Red Army approached their airfield. The exhausted survivors had pulled back to Voroshilovgrad by December 22 and among the unit's remaining aircraft was GD+CJ.

HENSCHEL HS 129 B-2 ▶

Operation Pugilist, followed by Operation Supercharge II, in March 1943 succeeded in outflanking German forces holding what was known as the Mareth Line in Tunisia. As British forces rolled through the Tebaga Gap, Allied air superiority was near-total. At the beginning of the year, 8./SchG 2 had been tasked with operating behind German lines in Tunisia to destroy any Allied armoured units that broke through the overstretched front line. However, even with substantial escort the Hs 129s were vulnerable. Red C of 8./SchG 2 was one of three shot down by flak on March 27, 1943.

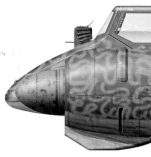

HENSCHEL HS 129 B-2 ◄

The Hs 129 was particularly ill-suited to desert operations but this was not discovered until after 4./SchlG 2 had been hastily deployed to North Africa during November 1942. The Hs 129's Gnome-Rhone engines had overheated during operations on the Eastern Front but in a hot climate they could barely be kept functional. Not long after the unit's first operation from El Adem in Tunisia, two sandstorms wrecked havoc on the Hs 129s' engines. By the end of December, most of the aircraft were wrecked and the unit's personnel were transferred back to the Eastern Front. This is Blue C, WNr. 0297 of 4./SchlG 2, as it appeared at El Adem in December 1942.

HENSCHEL HS 129 B-2 ◄

White Chevron with Blue O, WNr. 0310, was flown by Hauptmann Bruno Mayer of 4.(Pz)/SchlG 2 during December 1942 from El Adem in Tunisia. It features the regulation Mediterranean white band on its rear fuselage and has both a white chevron and metal Staffelkapitän's pennant on its aerial mast. Mayer's unit was formed specifically for anti-tank operations and the aircraft's camouflage was applied at the factory. Mayer himself would finish the war having flown more than 500 missions.

HENSCHEL HS 129

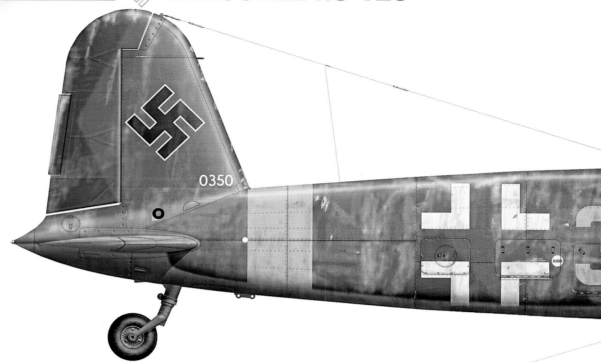

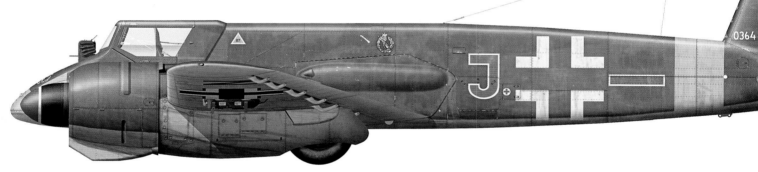

cooling, better sand and dust filters were added, the fuel system was improved, a slimmer mid-fuselage antenna replaced the original wider one and the landing light on the port wing was removed from the design. The first H-2 was produced in May 1942 and the following month the RLM ordered another 928 examples – which would bring the overall number of Hs 129s up to 1008 including all prototypes and development aircraft.

The last production version of the Hs 129 was the B-3. This was essentially a B-2 fitted with a huge BK 7.5 installed under its fuselage – making the Hs 129 capable of penetrating the armour of any tank in the world. However, only a handful of B-3s were produced, a small number being made at Henschel's factory and the remainder being upgraded from B-2 to B-3 standard. Estimates on the number created vary from fewer than 20 to as many as 25.

It is beyond the scope of this publication to detail the many equipment packs produced for the Hs 129, but in the field it proved itself to be one of the most adaptable, rugged and capable aircraft operated by the Luftwaffe. ●

HENSCHEL HS 129 B-2 ▲

Oberleutnant George Dornemann of 4.(Pz)/SchlG 1 flew Blue Chevron with Blue H on July 13, 1943, during the Battle of Kursk. The day before, the Soviets had launched a counterattack, Operation Kutusov, against the rear of the German forces on the northern side. The Red Army had overwhelming numbers on its side – with six Soviet rifle divisions attacking two German infantry regiments. The line collapsed and the Soviet units advanced 23km into the German flank. On the 13th the Hs 129s of 4.(Pz)/SchlG 1 entered the fray but by this stage the Soviet offensive included 1.2 million men, 2400 tanks and 26,000 artillery pieces and there was little they could do.

HENSCHEL HS 129 B-2 ▼

Pz.Jä.St./JG 51 operated Hs 129s, including Yellow 3, in support of the retreating Army Group South from Poltava in the Ukraine during the spring of 1943.

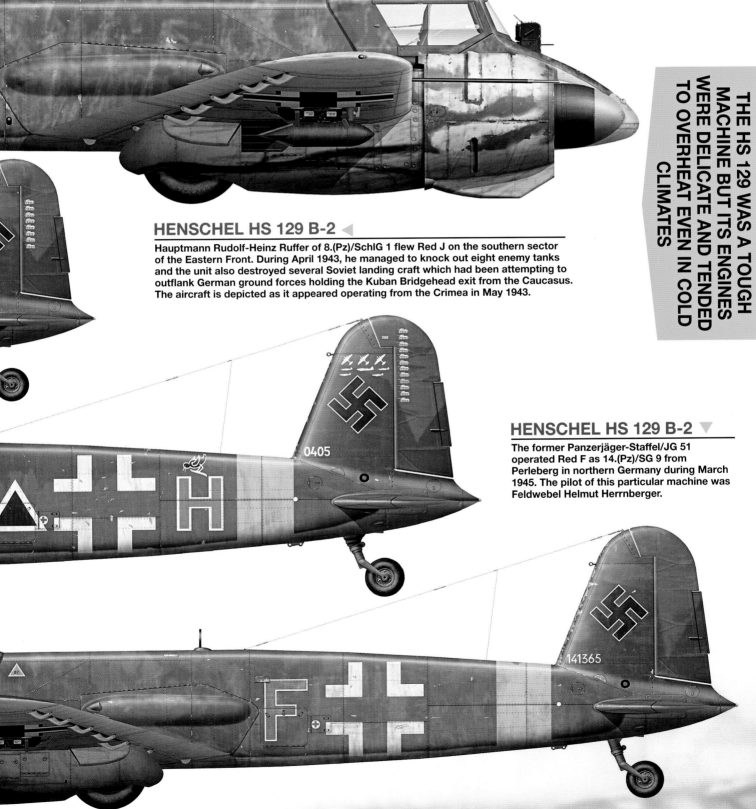

HENSCHEL HS 129 B-2 ◄

Hauptmann Rudolf-Heinz Ruffer of 8.(Pz)/SchlG 1 flew Red J on the southern sector of the Eastern Front. During April 1943, he managed to knock out eight enemy tanks and the unit also destroyed several Soviet landing craft which had been attempting to outflank German ground forces holding the Kuban Bridgehead exit from the Caucasus. The aircraft is depicted as it appeared operating from the Crimea in May 1943.

HENSCHEL HS 129 B-2 ▼

The former Panzerjäger-Staffel/JG 51 operated Red F as 14.(Pz)/SG 9 from Perleberg in northern Germany during March 1945. The pilot of this particular machine was Feldwebel Helmut Herrnberger.

THE HS 129 WAS A TOUGH MACHINE BUT ITS ENGINES WERE DELICATE AND TENDED TO OVERHEAT EVEN IN COLD CLIMATES

DORNIER DO 217

A big step forward from the Do 17, Dornier's Do 217 was nevertheless a lacklustre medium bomber able to fulfil many different roles while not being particularly good at any of them.

1940-1945

When a requirement was issued in early 1938 for a twin-engined bomber, reconnaissance, and smoke-laying machine, Dornier responded with the Do 217. This was based on the already successful Do 17 but was to be powered by a pair of DB 601 Bs. It would benefit from a more capacious fuselage than its predecessor, carrying up to 1500kg in bomber form – compared to the Do 17 Z's 1000kg – or more fuel plus two cameras in recce form. And as a smoke-layer, it would carry two S200 smoke generators.

Not long after this triple-role machine was drawn up, a revised Do 217 with floats was considered as a heavy naval dive-bomber but this came to nothing while the triple-role Do 217 was the

subject of a development contract. A mock-up had been built, inspected and approved by July 1938, with the Do 217 V1 being very rapidly constructed thereafter. It made its first flight on October 4, 1938, but while its handling capabilities were being tested on October 11, one of its engines failed and it was destroyed in a crash. However, the V2 was ready to fly on November 5 and commenced a series of dive tests.

The V3, first flown on February 25, 1939, was powered by Jumo 211 A-1s, as was the V4. Tests on the V5, fitted with Jumo 211 B-1s, got under way on June 22, 1939. Rather than commencing full

DORNIER DO 217 E-4 ▲

Operating from Amsterdam-Schiphol in Holland during early 1942, 7./KG 2 flew anti-shipping operations in the English Channel This is one of the unit's aircraft, U5+ZR, as it appeared in April 1942.

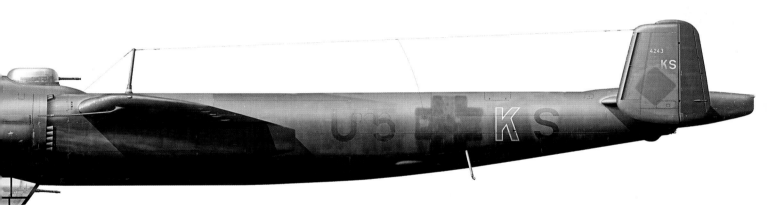

DORNIER DO 217 E-4 ▲

U5+KS WNr. 4243, of 8./KG 2, as it appeared in May 1942 when the unit was being readied for night operations. This particular aircraft took part in a raid on the Rolls-Royce plant in Derby on July 27, 1942.

DORNIER DO 217 E-4 ▲

U5+FN, W.Nr. 5532 as it appeared flown by Oberfeldwebel Brendebach of 5./KG 2, based at Eindhoven, Holland, on August 19, 1942. Piloted by Hauptmann Hermann Euler, the same aircraft was shot down by an RAF Beaufighter of 125 Squadron near Beaminster in Dorset at 10.30pm on February 16, 1943. Euler and all his crew were killed.

production with the Do 217 A-series, the A, B, C and E types were all worked on simultaneously during this time.

The Do 217 A was a DB 601 F-powered reconnaissance version fitted with two cameras in a jettisonable equipment pack, while the Do 217 B was to be a Jumo 211 B-powered bomber fitted with dive brakes. The Do 217 C was to be a bomber powered by the BMW 801.

While some examples of the Do 217 A-0 series were completed, the B-series was cancelled and the C-series was earmarked for the Jumo 211 B instead. It appears as though the Do 217 D did exist as a project but little is known about it and it never advanced to prototype construction.

Only a handful of Do 217 As and Cs were built before Dornier refocused its attention on the next in line – the E-series.

The specification under which the early Do 217s had been designed was revised on July 8, 1939, with a requirement that the type should be capable of launching glide bombs during either maritime or land-based operations. It also had to be capable of diving at a 50-degree angle.

The first Do 217 E-0 pre-production aircraft made its maiden flight on October 1, 1940, powered by a pair of BMW 801 A engines. Armament of the E-1 was to consist of a single MG 151 cannon firing forward and five MG 15s on gimbal mounts within the cockpit. Two were positioned to the upper rear, firing over the tail fin, two more fired beneath the fuselage and to the rear, while the remaining gun was mounted in a chin position.

This was quickly followed by the E-3 version, which offered improved armour for the crew and replaced the 15mm MG 151 with a 20mm MG FF. The E-2, having been worked on in parallel, arrived slightly later and incorporated a new EDL 131 electrically actuated dorsal turret as well as uprated BMW 801 L engines. Two of the MG 15s were replaced by MG 131s. Some early E-1s were later upgraded to E-2 standard.

The E-4 level bomber was then produced, which was similar to the E-2 in most respects but with the dive

DORNIER DO 217 E-4 ▼

Taking off from Soesterberg in Holland in bad weather on December 16, 1942, II./KG 40, including F8+DM of 4./KG 40, attacked a string of targets across the south of England.

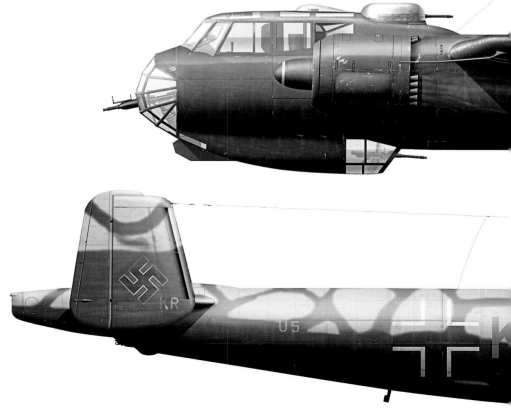

DORNIER DO 217 E-2 ▼

Another anti-shipping Do 217 operating out of Holland was F8+FN of 5./KG 40, based at Soesterberg during August 1942.

DORNIER DO 217 E-1 ▲

With Operation Anton, the Germans finally occupied Vichy France on November 10, 1942. Aircraft such as U5+BR of 7./KG 2, based at Bordeaux-Merignac, France, were required to wear white wing bands for the operation. Anton was completed within a day, since the nominally independent puppet-state French lacked the military resources to resist.

DORNIER DO 217 K-1 ▼

Flown by Leutnant Gunther Wolff of 7./KG 2 on a bombing raid targeting Lincoln on January 15, 1943, U5+KR was shot down by a night fighter Mosquito of 151 Squadron. The Dornier dived into the ground at Boothby Graffoe, Lincolnshire, at 8.50pm and all on board were killed.

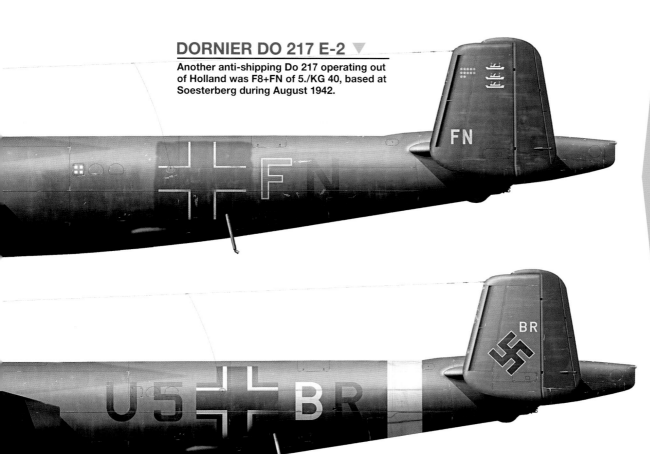

DORNIER DO 217 K-1 ▶

On the night of May 4/5, 1943, an RAF Mosquito night fighter flown by F/O Brian Williams of 605 Squadron shot down U5+AA, WNr. 4415, flown by Leutnant Ernst Andres of the Stab./KG 2 based at Landsmeer, Holland. The aircraft was destroyed near Eindhoven.

DORNIER DO 217 K-1 ▼

This aircraft K7+EK, WNr. 4519, was flown by the training and replacement unit 2./Erg.Sta (F) N from Orscha-Süd in the USSR during May 1943.

THE K AND M-SERIES MACHINES WERE THE SAME EXCEPT FOR THEIR ENGINES - BMW 801S AND DB 603S RESPECTIVELY

brakes removed and Kutonase barrage balloon cutters built into the leading edges of its wings. The E-5 was the much anticipated glide bomb-carrying version. It was modified to accept a single Henschel Hs 293 or drop tank under each of its outer wing sections and the cockpit was fitted out with the missile's associated radio guidance and control system.

By 1942, it had been hoped that the He 177 would finally be able to take over from the Do 217 as a glide bomb and guided weapons carrier but the He 177 was continuing to suffer severe engine problems. In addition, there was an urgent need for more night fighters to combat RAF raids, which were growing in frequency, so it was decided that the Do 217 would need to continue in service.

A major upgrade of the existing design was set in motion and while new night fighter versions were created as the J-series, new bombers were created as the K-series and M-series – the former powered by BMW 801s and the latter by DB 603s. The reason for specifying two versions in parallel with two different engines was to insure against the supply of either one drying up.

In both cases, the original cockpit was replaced by a more streamlined new 'stepless' design. This had a single large 'bulb' of glazing covering the upper front of the nose, rather than the separate nose glazing and windscreen arrangement seen on earlier models. The first Do 217 fitted with this layout, a modified E-2 which kept its BMW 801s, began flight tests on March 31, 1942, and the full production version, the Do 217 K-1 night bomber went into production six months later.

The K-1 retained the BMW 801 L but was slightly faster than its predecessors

due to its cleaner aerodynamic shape. For defence, it had two MG 81 Zs in its nose, two MG 81s or MG 81 Zs in sideways-facing positions, an MG 131 in a DL 131/1C dorsal turret and a second one in a WL 131/1 position facing rearwards on its gondola. The second K-series machine, the K-2, was an anti-shipping machine specifically modified to carry the Fritz X guided bomb. Up to two of these 1362kg weapons could be mounted beneath the aircraft's inner wings – although performance suffered dramatically of more than one was carried at a time. Overall wing area was increased in order to help overcome this problem.

Another unique feature of the Do 217 K-2 was an MG 81 Z installed at the very end of its tail. This had 350 rounds and could be targeted using a backwards-looking periscope in the cockpit. However, it was fixed in position and the pilot had to turn the aircraft itself in order to be able to aim it. It was relatively ineffective and could be jettisoned to reduce weight if necessary.

The final K-series machine, the K-3, was another anti-shipping aircraft with improved guidance systems which could be used with either Fritz X bombs or

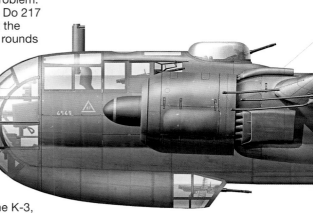

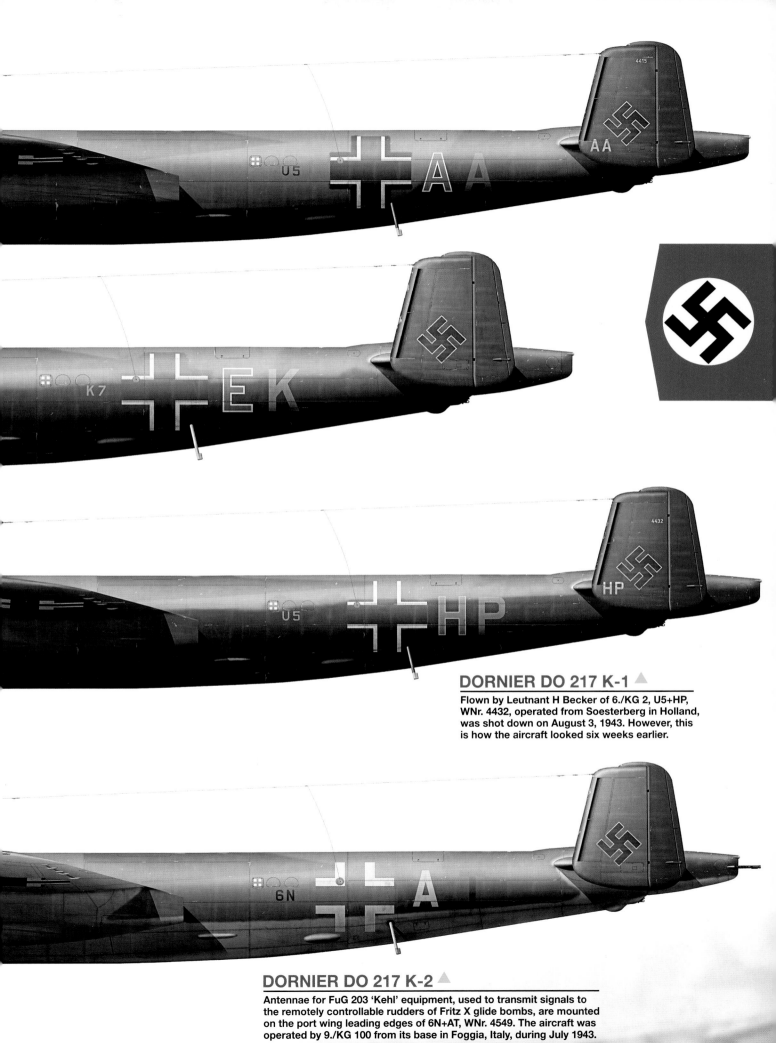

DORNIER DO 217 K-1 ▲

Flown by Leutnant H Becker of 6./KG 2, U5+HP,
WNr. 4432, operated from Soesterberg in Holland,
was shot down on August 3, 1943. However, this
is how the aircraft looked six weeks earlier.

DORNIER DO 217 K-2 ▲

Antennae for FuG 203 'Kehl' equipment, used to transmit signals to
the remotely controllable rudders of Fritz X glide bombs, are mounted
on the port wing leading edges of 6N+AT, WNr. 4549. The aircraft was
operated by 9./KG 100 from its base in Foggia, Italy, during July 1943.

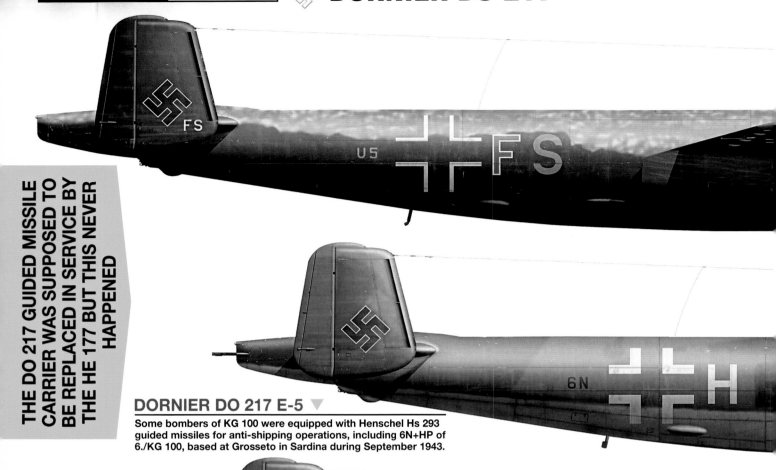

DORNIER DO 217 E-5 ▼

Some bombers of KG 100 were equipped with Henschel Hs 293 guided missiles for anti-shipping operations, including 6N+HP of 6./KG 100, based at Grosseto in Sardina during September 1943.

Hs 293 missiles. It retained the larger wings of the K-2 and could be fitted with standard bombing racks to carry a normal bomb load. Only a small number of K-3s were built since the Fw 190 also required BMW 801 engines and was given a higher priority.

Meanwhile, the M was worked on in parallel with the K and the first prototype M, also based on a modified E-2, was flown on June 16, 1942 – 10 weeks after the K prototype. Like the K-1, the M-1 was a night bomber and was similar in most respects to its radial-engined stablemate. The type enjoyed a production run of 438 examples, compared to just 220 K-1s. The M-3 was equivalent to the K-3 and the M-5 was a dedicated Hs 293 missile carrier.

From its entry into service during 1941 until the end of the war, the Do 217 was only ever available in comparatively low numbers. Employed on standard bombing and anti-shipping missions mostly in Western Europe, its workmanlike performance was never outstanding and the units which operated it tended to suffer heavy losses owing to the type's vulnerability in the face of advanced mid-to-late war Allied fighters. ●

DORNIER DO 217 M-1 ▼

Having suffered damage during a raid on the night of February 22, 1944, U5+DK, WNr. 56051, flown by Oberfeldwebel H Steman of 2./KG 2, was forced to make a belly landing in allotments behind 302 Milton Road, Cambridge, at 10.40pm. The aircraft was substantially intact and provided the British with a wealth of information about the type.

DORNIER DO 217 E-4 ▼

Painted up for night operations, U5+FS was flown by pilots of 8./KG 2 from Gilze Rijen, Holland, during September 1943.

DORNIER DO 217 K-2 ▼

An armistice was agreed between the Allies and the Italians in early September 1943 which included the stipulation that the Italian fleet and all Italian aircraft would be transferred immediately to places chosen by the Allied command. An Italian navy battlegroup in the Mediterranean which included the powerful battleship *Roma* moved to Malta in order to surrender on September 9 and was set upon by KG 100's bombers, including 6N+HR flown by 19-year-old Leutnant Klaus Deumling of 7./KG 100. During the assault, a Fritz X bomb dropped by Deumling – flying straight and level 7000m up – hit the *Roma* and together with a second bomb launched by another bomber, sank it. The ship turned upside down, broke into two parts and went down with two admirals, 86 officers and 1264 sailors.

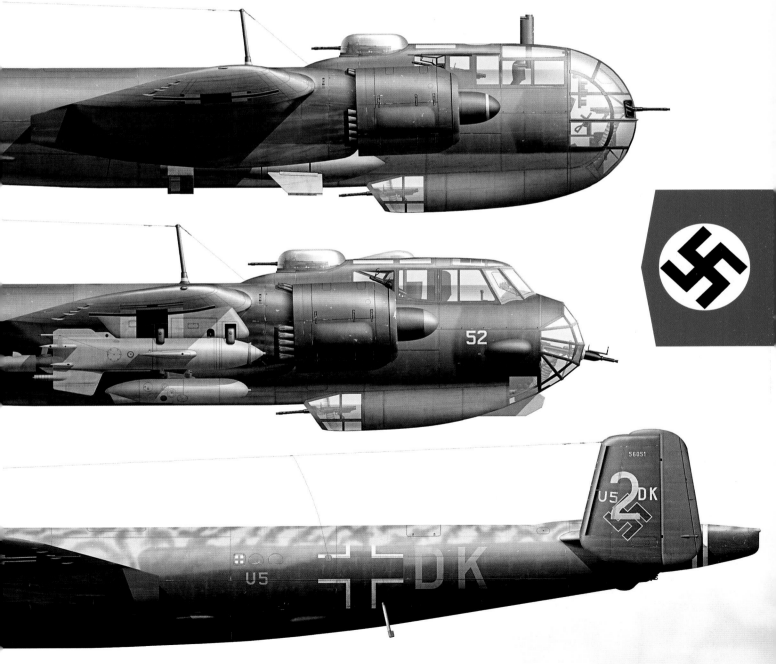

JUNKERS JU 188 E-1 ▼

During October 1943, KG 6's squadrons were deployed to airfields across northern France and Belgium ready to take part in Operation Steinbock – the so-called Baby Blitz which saw 474 Luftwaffe bombers pounding the Greater London area during the first half of 1944. Among the aircraft earmarked for the attack was 3E+IL of 3./KG 6, based at Chievres in Belgium in October 1943.

JUNKERS JU 188

With striking looks and a choice of good engines, the Ju 188 looked like a logical step forward from the Ju 88 but in truth it offered few advantages over developed versions of the older type.

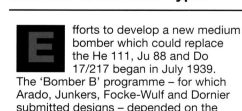

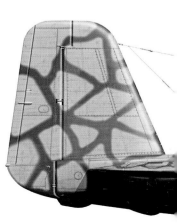

1941-1945

Efforts to develop a new medium bomber which could replace the He 111, Ju 88 and Do 17/217 began in July 1939. The 'Bomber B' programme – for which Arado, Junkers, Focke-Wulf and Dornier submitted designs – depended on the development of powerful new engines, particularly the Jumo 222 and DB 604 which were expected to develop 2000-2500hp each.

The programme continued until 1942, when it became clear that neither engine was going to reach full production. A new medium bomber was urgently needed, however, so existing types and more moderate development proposals were re-examined to see whether a suitable stopgap design could be put together.

Two years earlier, Junkers had begun testing a version of the Ju 88 powered by a pair of BMW 801 engines as the Ju 88 B. This also incorporated an entirely new forward fuselage and cockpit section characterised by a huge area of framed glass panels in front of and above the crew for improved visibility and a more efficient aerodynamic form.

The first B-series prototype had the same fuselage and tail surfaces as the Ju 88 A-1 – which meant that despite the increased power offered by its BMW 801 A/B engines the aircraft could only carry the same internal bomb load as the A-1. A series of 10 pre-production Ju 88 B-0s based on the longer-winged A-4 were delivered during the summer of 1940 with a slightly stretched cockpit in order to shift

the centre of gravity. While crews liked the B-0's cockpit, the design attracted no further orders and was shelved. Some of the 10 existing airframes were stripped of their bomb gear, fitted with extra internal fuel tanks and used for reconnaissance, while the remainder were kept by Junkers for use in development work.

When an alternative to Bomber B was required, Junkers took the opportunity to resubmit the Ju 88 B and the RLM commissioned a pair of prototypes for evaluation as the Ju 188. The Ju 188 V1 had originally been built to Ju 88 A-4 specification as the Ju 88 V44 and was

subsequently refitted with the new cockpit and a new tail fin.

After flight testing and inspection, an order was finally placed for the Ju 188 in October 1942. The second prototype was delivered in January 1943 and was used to establish a layout where either BMW 801 G or Jumo 213 A engines could be fitted interchangeably, depending on which engine type was available.

While the prototypes were armed with MG 131s, the production type Ju 188 had MG 151/20 cannon in its nose and dorsal turrets.

In order to differentiate between the two, Jumo 213-powered examples were designated Ju 188 A and aircraft fitted

JUNKERS JU 188 A-2 ▼

U5+KH, WNr. 160096 of 1./KG 2, was stationed at Bron in France during February-March 1944 as Operation Steinbock proceeded against Britain.

JUNKERS JU 188 E-1 ▼

After less than two months of operations over Britain, KG 6 was seriously depleted. By March 20, I. KG 6 had only 13 Ju 188s left and only 10 of them were serviceable. After another gruelling assault on the night of March 21/22, the unit was withdrawn from operations for six weeks for rest and refitting. 3E+LL of 3./KG 6 is depicted as it appeared at Melsbroek in Belgium during late March 1944.

THE FIRST VERSION OF THE JU 188 TO BE DELIVERED WAS THE JU 188 E, WHICH ONLY DIFFERED FROM THE 'A' IN ITS ENGINES

with the BMW 801 were designated Ju 188 E. Therefore, contrary to the usual alphabetical coding sequence, the first Ju 188s to be delivered were all Es, with the first As following later and at a slower rate.

Production began with the E-1 in February 1943 and the type entered operational service that August. A total of 283 had been constructed by the beginning of 1944.

At this point, deliveries of the A-2 commenced – which differed from the A-1 in having MW50 methanol-water injection built into its Jumo 213s. An anti-shipping version of the Ju 188 was also produced at this time, fitted with FuG 200 radar and torpedo dropping gear. Fitted with the Jumo 213 it was the Ju 188 A-3 and with the BMW 801 it was the E-2.

There was no Ju 188 B, to avoid confusion with the Ju 88 B, so the Ju 188 C was intended to be the next production version after the A and E. This featured a new remote-controlled FA 15 tail turret incorporating a pair of MG 131s. The aircraft's cockpit equipment was augmented with a double-periscope system so that this could be aimed and fired by the crew. Only a single example was produced – by retrofitting the turret to a Ju 188 A-1 – before the variant was cancelled.

Reconnaissance versions of the A and E were created as the D and F respectively. Again, these were created by modifying existing aircraft. The bomb aimer and forward gun positions were removed from the cockpit and extra fuel tanks were added to improve range.

Further plans for the Ju 188 included the G- and H-series, which would have

JUNKERS JU 188 E-1 ▶

Leutnant Hans Altrogge of 5./KG 66 flew this aircraft, Z6+TN, from Montdidier in France during June 1944. Altrogge was a specialised pathfinder, using flares to mark out targets ahead of raids.

featured a fuselage modification enabling the aircraft to carry a greater bomb load. Neither of these entered production. A total of 283 Ju 188 As and Es were built during 1943 with a further 793 following in 1944. The type was then developed into the Ju 388.

Although it was only ever intended as a stopgap measure, the Ju 188 nevertheless offered only a scant improvement over the existing Ju 88 series. ●

JUNKERS JU 188 A-3/TROP ▶

Equipped as a torpedo-bomber, 1H+BD, WNr. 0342 had been flown by pilots of Stab III./KG 26 from Gardemoen, Norway, but it is shown here as it was surrendered to the British during early May 1945.

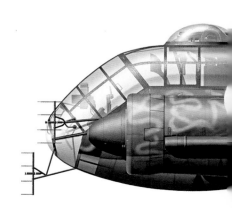

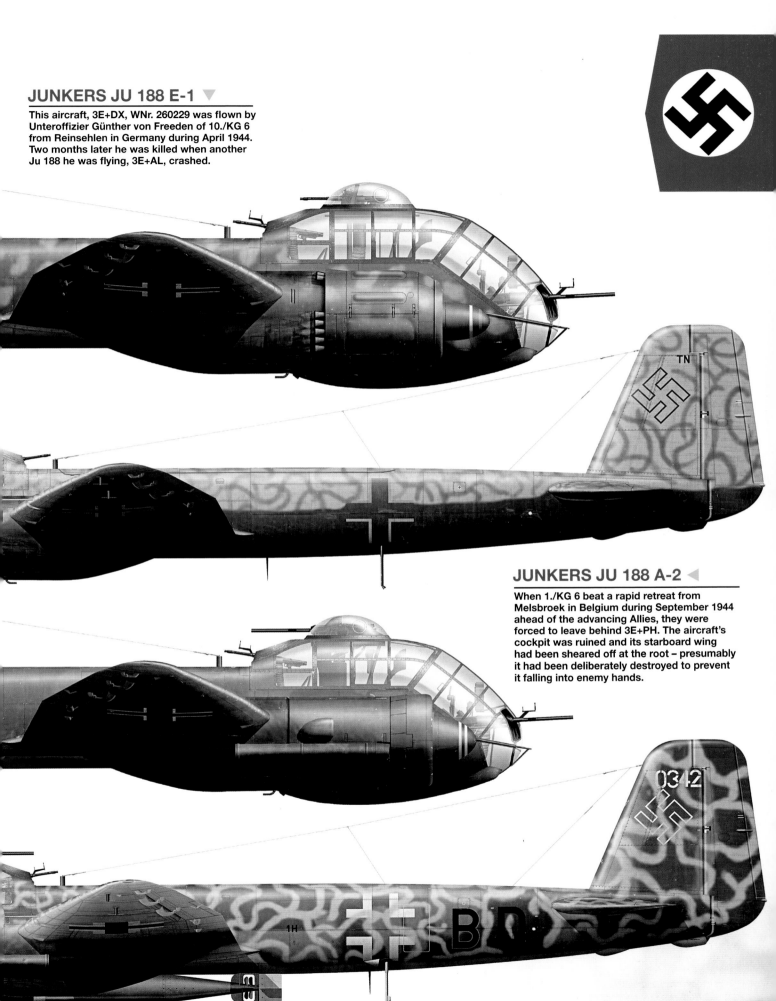

JUNKERS JU 188 E-1 ▼

This aircraft, 3E+DX, WNr. 260229 was flown by Unteroffizier Günther von Freeden of 10./KG 6 from Reinsehlen in Germany during April 1944. Two months later he was killed when another Ju 188 he was flying, 3E+AL, crashed.

JUNKERS JU 188 A-2 ◄

When 1./KG 6 beat a rapid retreat from Melsbroek in Belgium during September 1944 ahead of the advancing Allies, they were forced to leave behind 3E+PH. The aircraft's cockpit was ruined and its starboard wing had been sheared off at the root – presumably it had been deliberately destroyed to prevent it falling into enemy hands.

MESSERS
ME 262

MESSERSCHMITT ME 262 A-2A ▼

During the last three months of 1944, small formations of Me 262s flown by KG(J) 51 managed to keep RAF Tempest units tied down flying defensive patrols. One of these was 9K+YH of 1./KG 51. It had a slightly different style of camouflage on each side and the style of its large letter 'Y' was highly unusual.

Famous as the first jet fighter to see front line service, plans to also use the Me 262 for dropping bombs were drawn up almost as soon as the first production contract was awarded.

1939–1945

Both Heinkel and Messerschmitt received development contracts to design a twin-engine jet-propelled fighter towards the end of 1938, and by the summer of 1939 both firms' designs had reached the mock-up stage.

The mock-ups were inspected in December 1939 and each company received an order to construct a series of prototypes. Heinkel's design would go on to be given the RLM designation He 280 while Messerschmitt's project, P 65 and later P 1065, would become the Me 262.

The former was a tricycle undercarriage design propelled by Heinkel's own turbojets, designed in-house, while the latter was a tail-sitter powered by a pair of BMW P 3304 turbojets, as

shown in a company brochure headed Projektbaubeschreibung P 1065 Nr. 3, dated March 1940.

Engine difficulties hampered both companies and while Heinkel was able to begin towed flight testing towards the end of 1940, Messerschmitt was forced to test its Me 262 V1 airframe by fitting it with a nose-mounted Jumo 210 G piston engine.

During early 1942, however, 10 prototypes of the BMW P 3302, V1 to V10, were delivered to Messerschmitt and Me 262 V1 was modified to accept a pair of them. Its first powered flight was on March 25, 1942, but this was cut short when the first two P 3302s both suffered compressor blade failure.

Tests ended in April but on June 1 a pair of Jumo T1 turbojets were delivered

CHMITT

and over the next six weeks these were fitted to Me 262 V3. On July 18, the aircraft was flown for 12 minutes without problems in the morning, it then flew for another 13 minutes at around midday, managing to reach 342mph.

The Me 262 V3's sustained success with its Jumo T1s, the engine later being given the RLM designation 004, was the first real evidence that all the time, effort, money and, above all, faith, invested in jet fighters was going to pay off. A series of 30 pre-production aircraft was ordered in October 1942, which were to be built with

a tricycle undercarriage arrangement.

On March 4, 1943, a meeting was held to review the armament of the Me 262 and it was suggested that the originally proposed trio of MG 151 20mm cannon should be replaced with six MK 108 cannon or two MK 108s and a pair of MG 151s.

Five days later, and with news that a new lighter version of the Jumo 004 was nearing completion, the decision was taken to cancel Heinkel's He 280 and press ahead with the Me 262 as the Luftwaffe's first mass-produced jet fighter.

It appears to have been at this point that a fighter-bomber version of the Me 262 was first proposed. On March

25, 1943, Messerschmitt produced a report entitled 'Me 262 Jäger u. Jabo Kurzprojektbaubeschreibung'. The foreword of this document states that it is to supersede the previous descriptions dated March 1940 and November 20, 1942. Under 'weapons' the report states that "the armament of 3 x MG 151 will be replaced by one with 3cm weapons and a simultaneous increase in the number". Later this is clarified as: "a rigid armament of four MK 108 are in the weapons position. It is intended to accommodate two more MK 108 in the wing. As an alternative, the nose can be modified for the installation of three MG 151s or two MK 103s and one MG 151. The installation of two or four MG 131 in the wing as a replacement for the MK 108 may be possible, but has not been studied more closely."

It goes on to state: "Use as a Jabo [fighter bomber] with loads up to 500kg or 700kg is possible without modification. The possibility of hanging the bombs externally is planned from the outset."

The Me 262 was "primarily intended" to carry a single 500kg bomb but "the bomb system can be extended by use of a second attachment point to take 2 x 250kg bombs". A single BT 700 torpedo could also be carried, although "for centre of gravity reasons, two weapons must be removed from the top of the fuselage". Adolf Galland, General of Fighters, evaluated the Me 262 V4 on

MESSERSCHMITT ME 262 A-2A ▼

Five Spitfire IXb pilots from 401 Squadron RCAF claimed shared credit for shooting down 9K+BL, flown by Hauptmann Hans-Christoff Buttmann of 3./KG 51 from Rheine in Germany at 3pm on October 5, 1944. Buttmann is believed to have been killed after bailing out just 30m from the ground. An alternative account suggests that he actually bailed out at 610m but his parachute failed to open. The aircraft came down in a boggy field and created a hole 9m by 3.6m.

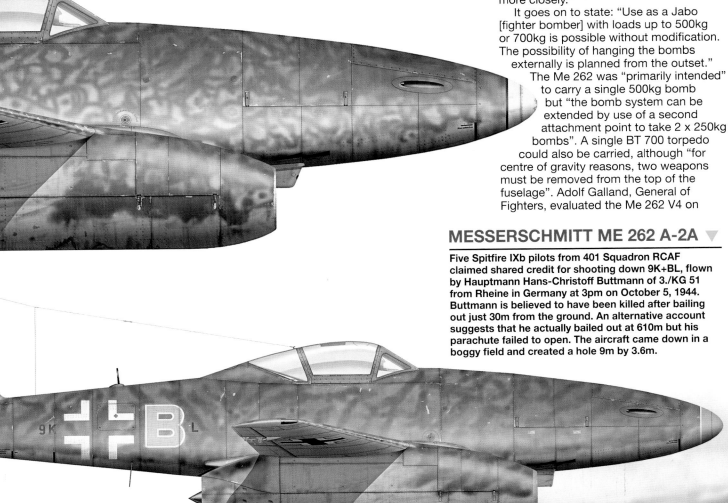

MESSERSCHMITT ME 262

THE ME 262 WAS PROPOSED AS A FIGHTER-BOMBER LONG BEFORE ADOLF HITLER PRONOUNCED THAT HE NEEDED THE AIRCRAFT TO CARRY BOMBS

MESSERSCHMITT ME 262 A-2 ▼

This aircraft, 9K+DH, WNr.500204, was flown by Feldwebel Karl-Albrecht Capitain of 1./KG 51, from Rheine, Germany. It is depicted as it appeared on February 21, 1945.

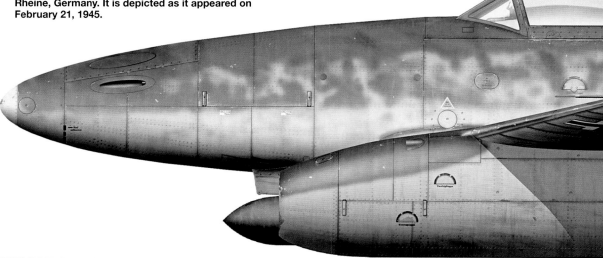

MESSERSCHMITT ME 262 A-2A ▼

Delivered to 1./KG 51 at Giebelstadt during mid-March 1945, this machine was flown operationally until mid-April. I./KG 51 was disbanded on April 24 and 12 or 13 of its remaining aircraft were delivered to the still-operational JV 44 at München-Riem. A few days later, however, I./KG 51 was re-formed and the aircraft were recovered with the intention of flying them to Prague. Only this one, 9K+FH, was left behind as unserviceable and was found by American troops a few days later by the edge of the autobahn south of Munich.

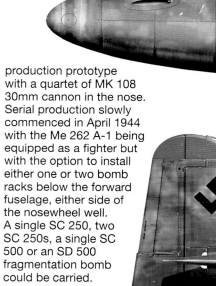

May 22, 1943 and famously reported to Reichsmarschall Hermann Göring that: "It flies as if there is an angel pushing." Nine days later, Göring officially declared that production of the Me 209 was to be suspended in favour of the Me 262.

Between July and August 1943, Messerschmitt's engineers and draftsmen worked on an array of designs showing how the basic Me 262 platform might be developed to perform a whole host of different tasks. The resulting report published on September 11, 1943, shows the standard Me 262 A-1 fighter compared against a fighter-bomber 'Jabo' version, three 'Schnellbomber' fast bomber versions, three 'Aufklärer' reconnaissance versions, three 'Interzeptor' interceptors and a 'Schulflugzeug' trainer version.

Me 262 V6, powered by a pair of Jumo 004 Bs, was the first Me 262 prototype to be fitted with a fully retractable tricycle undercarriage, and it made its first flight on October 17, 1943.

At a display of the Luftwaffe's latest experimental equipment on November 26 at Insterburg airfield, East Prussia, Hitler went to inspect the two Me 262s on show – V1 and V6. Indicating them, he said: "I'm not interested in this aircraft as a fighter. Can it carry bombs?"

Willy Messerschmitt assured him that it could – one 1000kg bomb or two 500kg bombs. Hitler then said: "At last, this is the aircraft I have been demanding for years. Here it is, but nobody recognised it. I order this aircraft be built as a bomber."

Me 262 V8 was completed on March 18 and was to be the A-series

production prototype with a quartet of MK 108 30mm cannon in the nose. Serial production slowly commenced in April 1944 with the Me 262 A-1 being equipped as a fighter but with the option to install either one or two bomb racks below the forward fuselage, either side of the nosewheel well. A single SC 250, two SC 250s, a single SC 500 or an SD 500 fragmentation bomb could be carried.

A dedicated fighter-bomber version, the Me 262 A-2a, was similar to the Me 262 A-1a in most respects except it carried two MK 108s in the nose rather than four, an extra 750 litre fuel tank in the rear fuselage and the ability to carry a wider range of bombs under its forward fuselage. It could still only carry loads up to 500kg, however. ●

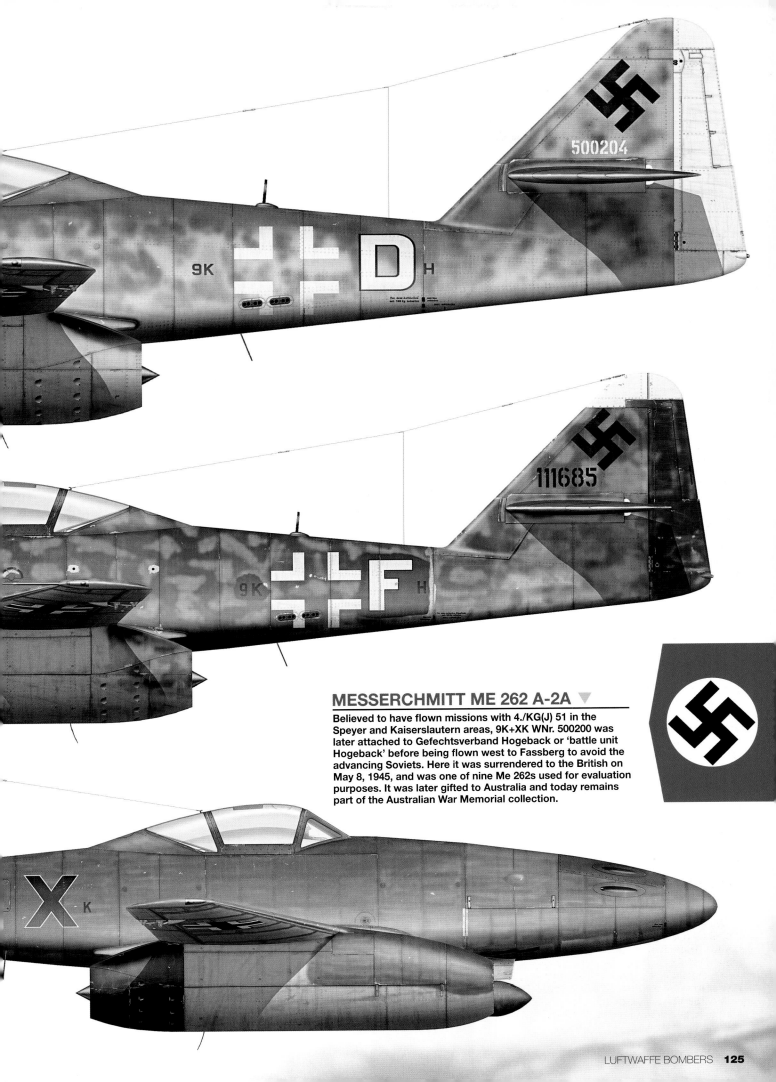

MESSERCHMITT ME 262 A-2A ▼

Believed to have flown missions with 4./KG(J) 51 in the Speyer and Kaiserslautern areas, 9K+XK WNr. 500200 was later attached to Gefechtsverband Hogeback or 'battle unit Hogeback' before being flown west to Fassberg to avoid the advancing Soviets. Here it was surrendered to the British on May 8, 1945, and was one of nine Me 262s used for evaluation purposes. It was later gifted to Australia and today remains part of the Australian War Memorial collection.

ARADO AR

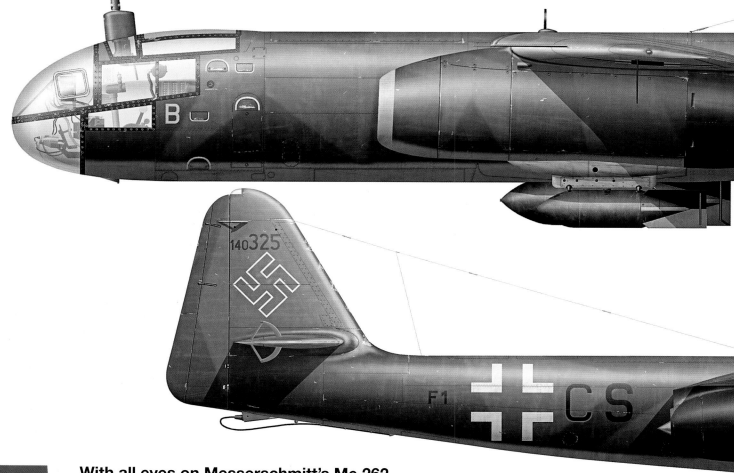

1941-1945

With all eyes on Messerschmitt's Me 262 as the Luftwaffe's first jet fighter, Arado quietly designed and built a jet reconnaissance platform which went on to become the world's first jet bomber.

Even as the competition to design a twin-jet fighter for the Luftwaffe was getting under way, there were already those who wondered whether turbojets might have wider applications.

Oberstleutnant Theodor Rowehl of the Aufklärungsgruppe Oberbefehlshaber der Luftwaffe (Ob. d. L.) – the reconnaissance wing of the commander-in-chief of the Luftwaffe – wanted a fast camera platform that could outrun enemy interceptors and quickly realised that jet engines might give him just that.

Since the early 1930s and under a variety of different names, Rowehl's unit had been secretly using specially prepared high-altitude aircraft, latterly the Ju 86 R, to carry out photo reconnaissance of defensive positions in France, Poland and the Soviet Union.

Following the outbreak of war in 1939, Rowehl urgently needed to undertake similar missions over Britain but knew that whatever aircraft his men used would need greater range and speed if they were to get their photos home safely. He approached the RLM in early 1940 to request a jet with the range to overfly any part of Britain, up to and including Scapa Flow, and the ministry agreed to have one developed for him.

Although Messerschmitt and Heinkel had already built up a little experience in

234

ARADO AR 234 B-2 ▲

The first Ar 234 unit to be declared operational was 9./KG 76 in mid-December 1944. Based at Münster-Handorf in Germany, the unit flew its first mission on Christmas Eve – bombing the city of Liege in Belgium in support of the Ardennes offensive. F1+BT was flown during the raid by 9./KG 76's commander Hauptmann Dieter Lukesch.

ARADO AR 234 B-2 ▲

This aircraft, F1+CS, WNr. 140325 of 8./KG 76, is depicted as it appeared at Burg in Germany during December 1944. The aircraft crashed and was destroyed on January 23, 1945.

designing jet aircraft by this point, asking either of them to undertake the design of a second jet would only have built further delays into what was already a difficult and protracted process.

Fortunately, however, the RLM had access to a team of capable and compliant designers at Arado. The company, based at Neuendorf, west of Brandenburg, had been nationalised as early as 1936 and was in the process of becoming a not-for-profit government-funded resources 'hub' available to provide additional capacity to the rest of Germany's aviation industry as required.

Arado maintain a design, development and aerodynamics staff for this purpose

and by giving Arado alone the design brief for a jet reconnaissance aircraft, rather than issuing an official requirement, the RLM neatly sidestepped all the problems of having to deal with Heinkel, Messerschmitt or any of the other aviation firms that were already struggling with their own designs.

Arado technical director Walter Blume was not thrilled by the prospect of having to develop a low volume high-flying jet-powered reconnaissance aircraft and handed the project to the company's 31-year-old head of aerodynamics Rüdiger Kosin and let him get on with it.

The project was given the company designation E 370 and initial design work

ranged across nine different layouts – some larger, some smaller, with different engine arrangements and wingspans. All featured a simple cigar-shaped fuselage with simple straight wings and cruciform tail.

It was decided to proceed with design E 370/IVa in October 1941. It was a single-seater that would be powered by a pair of BMW P 3302 engines (BMW 003), one under each wing, with a pair of Rb 50/30 or Rb 75/30 cameras positioned in the rear fuselage. There was to be a wooden skid rather than wheels as landing gear.

During three months of further design work, the E 370's fuselage was enlarged and its intended powerplant was switched to the more promising Jumo 004. A mock-up was commissioned in February 1942 and six prototypes were ordered in April. These were to have metal, rather than wooden, skids and there was to be an outrigger beneath each engine for added protection during a hard skid landing.

For ease of taxiing on the ground and take-off, a simple three-wheeled parachute-equipped dolly was devised. This would remain attached to the aircraft until shortly after take-off, when it would be jettisoned and would float safely back to earth under its parachute. Attachment points for rocket-assisted take-off units were also added to the Ar 234's wings just outboard of its engines.

The prototype order was increased to 20 in December 1942 and work on the

ARADO AR 234 B-2 ▼

Highly-decorated bomber pilot Major Hansgeorg Bätcher of Stab III./ KG 76 flew his final bombing mission of the war in F1+AD from Achmer, Germany, on February 21, 1945. Later that month he was appointed to lead the Me 262-equipped KG(J) 54, which he did until the end of the war.

Ar 234 V1 was completed in early 1943. However, engine delays meant its first flight was delayed until July 30, 1943. It remained aloft for 14 minutes having taken off without rocket assistance. The dolly was released at 2000ft but the parachute failed to open properly and was smashed to bits when it hit the ground. Further tests followed and Ar 234 V2 was ready by September.

By now, the RLM had become interested in the potential of the Ar 234 as a bomber. Arado was asked to design a version that could accommodate a bomb load but since the aircraft's narrow fuselage was almost entirely taken up with fuel tanks, the company's designers were forced to consider different ways of attaching a payload externally, with all the accompanying performance penalties from drag.

Furthermore, the experiments already conducted with the take-off dolly had persuaded the Ar 234's designers that the full production version would benefit from a fully retractable wheeled undercarriage and design work on this configuration quickly got under way. The skid version was designated Ar 234 A, while the wheeled undercarriage type became Ar 234 B.

Ar 234 V3 first flew on September 29, 1943, but the V2 was destroyed after a mid-air engine fire on October 1. On November 21, Ar 234 V3 formed part of a personal display of new technology for Adolf Hitler, alongside two Me 262s and a Me 163 B. Even though the Arado machine wasn't flown, the Führer liked it so much he ordered the company to build 200 examples, a mix of Ar 234 B-1 reconnaissance versions and Ar 234 B-2 bombers, before the end of 1944.

The first pre-production Ar 234 B-0 was completed in early June 1944 and first flew on June 8. Serial production of the Ar 234 B-2 bomber, the first full production type, began in July 1944 – following the completion of the first 20 pre-production Ar 234 B-0s.

The B-2 was capable of carrying a load of up to 1500kg (3307lb) externally. There was a bomb attachment point under each engine and another beneath the fuselage. Some 210 were built but an unknown number of these were converted to B-1 configuration. Several other bomber versions were proposed but none were built before the end of the war. ●

ARADO AR 234 B-2 ▼

Hit in the tail by anti-aircraft fire, F1+AS, WNr. 140589, flown by Feldwebel Friedrich Bruchlos of 8./KG 76, crashed on March 9, 1945. Bruchlos was killed and his body was not recovered from the wreckage until several decades later.

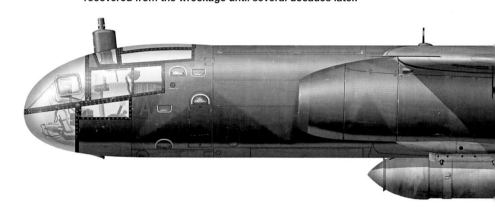

ARADO AR 234 B-2 ▶

Nine Ar 234s were surrendered to British forces at Stavanger-Sola, Norway, on May 5, 1945, including F1+HS, WNr. 140311 of 8./KG 76, which had just been flown there from Leck in Germany. The aircraft was later shipped to the US before being scrapped.

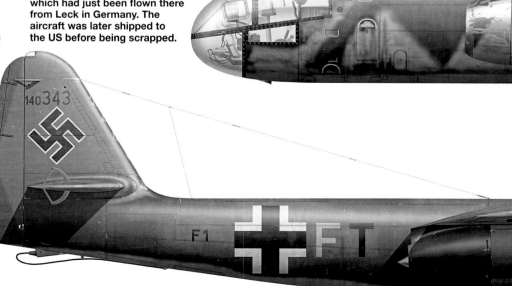